LOWER ELEMENTARY LEADER GUIDE

28 nineteen™
KIDS

Each week we achieve our goal of reaching kids and their families for Christ by making programming for children Fun, Intentional, Scriptural, and Helpful.

FUN

The fun level of our activities should reflect the fun level of our God. 28nineteen™ KIDS teaches God's Word in a way that is attractive and memorable to the children. God is not boring, and neither are we! And, if children have a great time, they will want to return ... with friends!

INTENTIONAL

We are intentional about knowing these children's names and needs. God hand-picked the children who attend your church every weekend. They are precious to Him, and they are precious to us! The focus of 28nineteen™ KIDS is always on reaching children and their families for Jesus Christ.

SCRIPTURAL

28nineteen™ KIDS is an unapologetically Bible based curriculum. In other words, we stand on the Word of God. All of our Bible Study and Worship lessons come directly from the Bible and teach our children straight biblical truth.

HELPFUL

Our goal is to teach children to be "doers of the Word, and not merely hearers" (James 1:22). To do this, we teach practical applications of biblical truths in each lesson. The children should leave with a challenge or an action to live their lives for Christ.

TABLE OF CONTENTS

LOWER ELEMENTARY BIBLE STUDY

MAIN POINT

The Bible is so rich! Every time we read a Bible story, be it the first or the fiftieth time, God can teach us something new. To help everyone stay on the same page, 28nineteen™ KIDS narrows in on one main point from the Bible story. Everything we do intentionally teaches the Bible story and this one point.

LEADER DEVOTION

The goal of the leader devotion is to help your leadership learn the lesson personally first. Secondly, our goal is to help your leadership feel an empowerment and excitement to share what they have learned with their classes. For this reason, each lesson begins with the same devotion for all leaders on an adult level. Background information, be it historical, cultural, or biblical, is incorporated to make the study richer in meaning for your leaders as well as for your kids. Additionally, the leader devotion helps your leadership team, be they Bible study teachers, worship leaders, or classroom helpers, to be on the same page.

ACTIVITIES

Actvities help kids stay engaged in the learning process while having fun. Each activity has a specific purpose and connects to the Bible lesson and main point for the day. Teachers can easily make this connection for themselves and their kids by reading the "Make the Connection" section below each activity.

- **Welcome Activities:** Many children find it difficult to walk into a group comfortably, thus it's helpful to have an activity that draws a child in and immediately gets them engaged. Welcome activities are designed to help all children feel they can confidently participate. These activities also serve as an introduction to the main point of the Bible lesson.

- **Crafts with Purpose:** 28nineteen™ KIDS does not have a craft for each lesson. Instead, crafts are included in lessons when they make sense and can be the most helpful to the kids as they learn.

- **Variety of Energy Levels:** Each lesson includes a variety of activities ranging in energy levels. Leaders can choose the activities that best fit the needs of their classes.

BIBLE LESSON

Bible lessons are clearly outlined into four sections: Intro, Read the Bible, Present the Gospel, and Application.

Intro: Short for "introduction," this section helps leaders grab kids' attention, quickly review past lessons, teach the overarching theme of the series, and get kids excited about the Bible story.

Read the Bible: Now we get to the good stuff! In this section, leaders encourage kids to read in the Bible as they discover God's Word for themselves.

Present the Gospel: The Bible is one big story, and it is all about Jesus! Each lesson seamlessly ties the Bible story to the truth of the Gospel. Leaders teach the truth of the Gospel and encourage kids to respond. Because we never know how many opportunities we will have to interact with each child, we never miss an opportunity to talk about Jesus.

Application: Our goal is to teach children to be "doers of the Word, and not merely hearers" (James 1:22). To do this, we teach practical applications of Biblical truths in each lesson. The children should leave with a challenge or an action to live their lives for Christ.

MEMORY VERSE

The goal of the memory verse activities is long-term understanding and memorization of Scripture. For this reason, 28nineteen™ KIDS focuses on one verse or passage during each series. Throughout the series, kids are encouraged to memorize these verses in fun and interactive ways. Just like the activities, each memory verse section has a "Make the Connection" section to help teachers explain the meaning and practical applications of the verses kids are memorizing.

STICKER STOP AND FRUIT OF THE SPIRIT STICKER POSTER

Cactus Corral uses several visual aids to help kids understand the abstract concept of the fruit of the Spirit. While not essential, stickers and posters are available at 28nineteencurriculum.com.

ALSO AVAILABLE

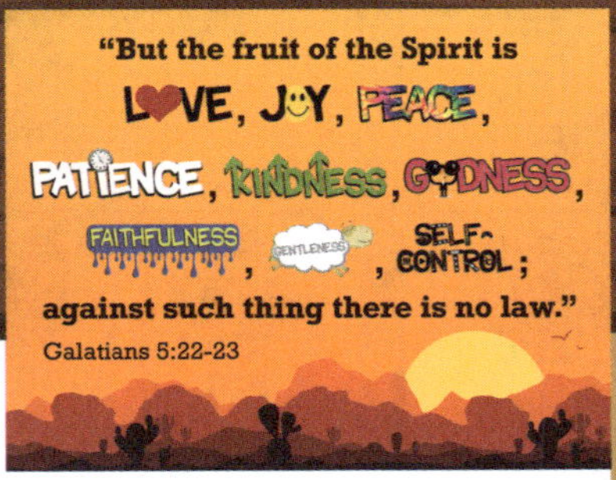

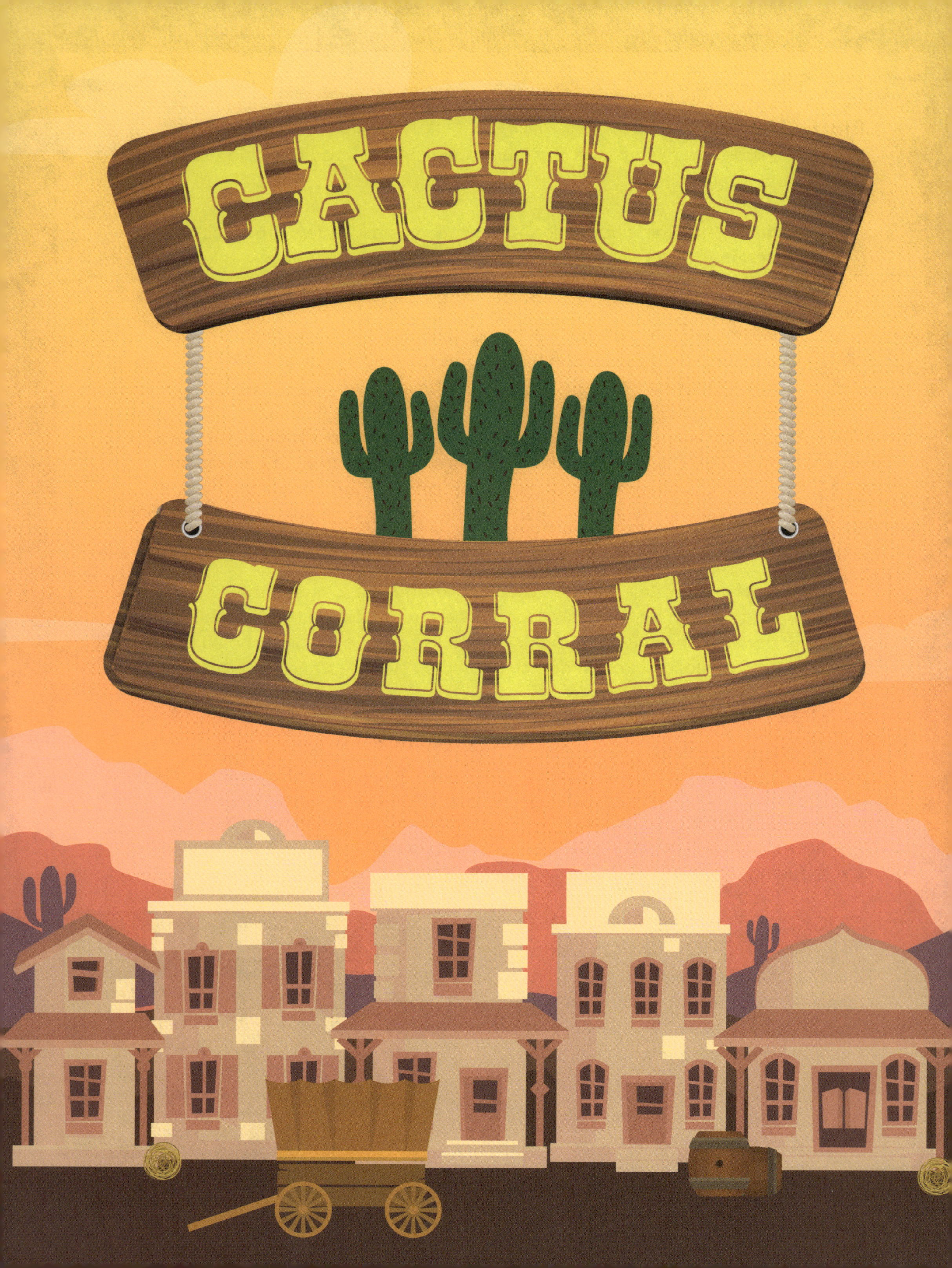
CACTUS
CORRAL

LESSON 1

MAIN POINT

God Shows Love,
so I Can Love Others.

BIBLE STORY

Peter Heals a Crippled Beggar.
(Acts 3 - 4:31)

MEMORY VERSE

"But the fruit of the Spirit is love, joy, peace, patience, kindness, goodness, faithfulness, gentleness, self control; against such things there is no law." Galatians 5:22-23 [NASB]

DON'T BE A PRICKLY PEAR!

SUPPLIES FROM THE GENERAL STORE

Craft:
Construction paper, Crayons, Markers

Activity 1:
Chairs

Bible Lesson:
Fruit of the Spirit poster (See page 5) and Love sticker

Activity 2:
None

Activity 3:
Pictures of different objects that could be used to show love like food, lawn mower, letters, etc. Anything that could be used to show someone you care will work fine. (one picture for each child)

Activity 4:
None

Memory Verse:
"Fruit of the Spirit" song (several versions of this song can be found online via YouTube and other streaming services), Music player

LEADER DEVOTION

READ

Acts 3 - 4:31

Peter and John were not wealthy men by the world's standards. However, they knew Jesus as their Lord and Savior and were filled with the spiritual and eternal wealth that comes from knowing God personally. In this account, they shared God's love by healing a man lame from birth. The beggar did not initially make eye contact, presumably because he knew it would not be returned. The more than forty years of feeling physically incomplete and frustrated with his situation ended abruptly, when he met Peter and John. Peter and John shared the gift Christ had given them: love. They made eye contact with him, made him physically whole through the power of God, and shared the Good News with him and all who would listen.

After Peter's sermon, Acts 4 tells us around five thousand men came to believe in Jesus as their Lord and Savior. Rather than accept the glory, the apostles gave the credit to Christ. The Sadducees, who did not believe in the resurrection from the dead, had Peter and John imprisoned in an effort to silence them. However, the Spirit cannot be silenced. Filled with the Spirit, Peter witnessed to the leaders, rulers, and even the high priest.

Acts 4:13 says, "The members of the council were amazed when they saw the boldness of Peter and John, for they could see that they were ordinary men with no special training in the Scriptures. They also recognized them as men who had been with Jesus."

Can people recognize you as having been with Jesus? The fruit of the Spirit is a product of knowing the Lord intimately, of spending time with Him. Do you give Him the opportunity to rub off on you as you spend time with Him? Take a quiet moment to recognize God's love. List all the ways the Lord has shown His love to the world and to you personally. List the ways God has shown His love to others through you. This first characteristic is also the most important fruit of the Spirit (1 Corinthians 13). Ask the Lord to teach you to love as He loves.

WELCOME

CRAFT: COWBOY POPPER

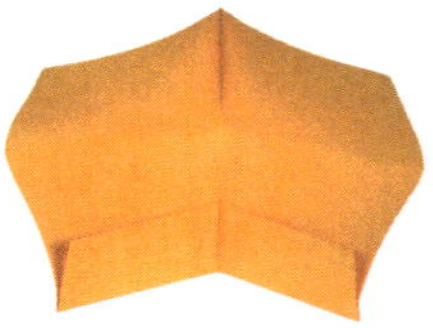

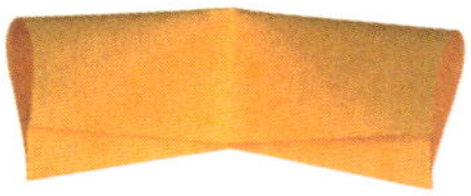

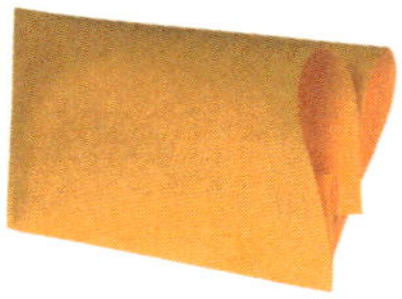

MATERIALS: Construction paper, Crayons, Markers

DIRECTIONS: Have kids decorate a regular sheet of 8.5" x 11" paper to look western. Lay the paper on the table landscape, then fold up about 1" from the bottom. Fold up, AGAIN, another inch. Then fold it in half (to make a square), keeping the previous folds on the outside. Pick up the popper holding it on the tip of the fold in the middle.

Fold the inner part most of the way down, creating two air pockets. (You should have 2 rounded pieces – do not crease this fold.) Hold the bottom right corners making sure the inner fold is loose and can easily slide. Then swing the popper down, so it can catch some air. After a few tries, you should get a loud pop.

CAMPFIRE CONNECTION:

Like a gong or a cymbal (1 Corinthians 13:1), the Cowboy Popper makes a loud noise that carries a long distance. When you stop moving it, it stops making noise. It takes action to make the loud noise.

- How do we show our families that we love them? Friends? Strangers?
- How do we show those people that God loves them?

If you were to swing the Cowboy Popper all day, your arm would get pretty tired, wouldn't it? We can't love others all the time, if we don't know the One who loves us more than we can imagine. God loves you SO much, and He will give you the strength to love others. Today we'll hear a really cool true story about how God gave Peter the power to show His love to someone in need.

ACTIVITY 1: DO YOU LOVE YOUR NEIGHBOR?

MATERIALS: Chairs

DIRECTIONS: Have kids put chairs in a big circle. One player, who will not need a chair, will stand in the center of the circle. The center person chooses someone in the circle to ask "Do you love your neighbor?" That person can answer either "yes" or "no." If the person answers "yes," everyone must switch seats, trying not to get stuck in the middle. If the person answers "no," the center person then asks, "Whom do you love?" The person can then answer something like "people with tennis shoes on," and everyone wearing tennis shoes must switch seats while trying not to get stuck in the middle.

CAMPFIRE CONNECTION:

That was a crazy game!!

- Did you like the game better when you got to switch seats or when you had to stay in your seat?

Games are more fun when you get to play a lot. The same is true in life. It's a lot more fun if we learn to include and love everyone around us – not just the people we know or like.

- What does the Bible say about loving other people? ***(Luke 10:25-29)***
- According to these verses, whom does God say we should love? *(everyone!)*
- Whom does God love? *(John 3:16 says He loves the whole world!)*

GOD SHOWS LOVE, SO I CAN LOVE OTHERS.

BIBLE LESSON

GOD SHOWS LOVE, SO I CAN LOVE OTHERS.

INTRO

MATERIALS: Finger paint, Finger paint paper (two sheets)

Place a glob of finger paint on one sheet of finger paint paper.

What will happen when I rub this blank sheet of paper onto the paper with paint? Right! The paint will rub off onto the blank sheet of paper. *Demonstrate by rubbing the papers together.*

When the papers get close together, they rub off on each other. Now they both have paint. The same thing happens when we spend time with friends, and when we spend time with God. Spending time around friends, or with God, "rubs off" on us. In Galatians 5:22-23, Paul talks about some of the ways knowing God shows up in our lives. He calls these things the fruit of the Spirit. For the next few weeks, we are going to learn about the fruit of the Spirit by studying some of the first Christians, the first people to have the Holy Spirit living inside of them. Today we are going to learn about the ways God's love rubs off on us.

LOVE

STICKER STOP

Place the Love Sticker on your Fruit of the Spirit poster *(See page 5).*

We don't have to do anything to make our hearts beat. They beat on their own. Loving others is different, because love is a choice. Love is something we say and something we do. We tell people we love them, and we show people we love them by the way we act and speak towards them.

- How does God show us that He loves us?

God loves us a lot! The book of Acts is a history book in the New Testament of the Bible about the first Christians and the early church. Today we are going to learn a true story from Acts 3-4. As we hear the story, listen for ways Peter and John showed God's love to others.

READ THE BIBLE

Read Acts 3:1-8.

- What did Peter and John do when they saw the beggar by the gate?
- How did they show the man God's love? *(looking at him directly, healing)*

Peter and John did not have money to give the man, but they did not give up or choose to ignore him. They decided to share the love of God with the man by healing him. Then they shared God's love with the man in a different way. They told him, and everyone around them, about Jesus.

PRESENT THE GOSPEL

Jesus is God's Son. Unlike us, Jesus never sinned. He never made even one wrong choice. You and I have all sinned. We have all chosen to do wrong, but Jesus never did. The Bible tells us in Romans 6:23 that the punishment for sin is death, separation from God. Jesus did not deserve to be punished, but chose to take the punishment we deserved. He died on a cross, but He did not stay dead. Jesus came back to life three days later! Because of Jesus, we can have a relationship with God. We can get to know Him as our God, our Friend, and our Boss. That is amazing! If you do not know what it means to have a relationship with God or have questions about what it means to be a Christian, please let us know. We would all love to tell you about Jesus.

READ THE BIBLE

Telling someone about Jesus is the most loving thing we can do, because we are actually sharing God with people. Unfortunately, not everyone will understand right away that Jesus is Lord. As Peter and John told people the Good News about Jesus and His love for us, a group of people became very angry. They did not believe Jesus had come back to life, and they did not like Peter and John telling the truth about Jesus. So, they put Peter and John in jail for the night.

Read Acts 4:4-7.

Peter and John told everyone about Jesus and His love for them. Even though they were put in jail for telling the truth about Jesus, five thousand men heard the truth and believed in Jesus. That is amazing! They told the leaders it was only because of Jesus that the lame man was healed. Listen closely to these next verses.

Read Acts 4:13-14.

The leaders knew Peter and John were friends with Jesus. Jesus had rubbed off on them. They were confident. Jesus had given them the power to heal the man and to speak boldly. Jesus had given them the power to love others, like He did, without being afraid of what anyone else thought of them.

APPLICATION

1 Corinthians 13: 1-7 says, "If I could speak all the languages of earth and of angels, but didn't love others, I would only be a noisy gong or a clanging cymbal. If I had the gift of prophecy, and if I understood all of God's secret plans and possessed all knowledge, and if I had such faith that I could move mountains, but didn't love others, I would be nothing. If I gave everything I have to the poor and even sacrificed my body, I could boast about it; but if I didn't love others, I would have gained nothing.

Love is patient and kind. Love is not jealous or boastful or proud or rude. It does not demand its own way. It is not irritable, and it keeps no record of being wronged. It does not rejoice about injustice but rejoices whenever the truth wins out. Love never gives up, never loses faith, is always hopeful, and endures through every circumstance."

In other words, we could be the most amazing people on the face of the earth, and it would mean nothing if we didn't have the love of God. Love is the first and most important fruit of the Spirit. When we spend time getting to know God, we start to understand how much He loves us and how much He loves other people.

1 John 3:18 says, "Dear children, let's not merely say that we love each other; let us show the truth by our actions." So I challenge you this week to really look at your life. How do you show God's love to your family? To your friends at school? To your teachers? To people you don't know? Ask God to help you see others the way He sees them, then show others God's love by the way you speak and act.

PRAY

ACTIVITY 2: ACTION VERB RELAY

MATERIALS: None

DIRECTIONS: Put kids into even teams. Have each team line up at one end of the room. You might want to create a starting line with masking tape to make sure everyone starts at the same place. When you say go, kids must run, one at a time, from the starting line to the opposite side of the wall and back. The first team to finish wins! Play this several times. Each time you play, get kids to do a different motion as they go to the opposite wall: skipping, jumping, crawling, crab walking, etc.

ACTIVITY OPTION:

For a fast-paced version of this game, hand out index cards with different action verbs on them to each child. Kids must follow the instructions on the card to get to the wall and back. Play it this way several times, allowing kids to switch cards each time.

CAMPFIRE CONNECTION:

That was fun! Each team did a great job! What do these words have in common: run, skip, jump, crawl? They are all action words. Each one of those words is something that people DO. "Love" is a verb, too. For example, in the sentence "I love you," love is the VERB. It is something that we DO.

- What is the difference between saying that you love someone and showing that you love someone?
- What kind of actions show love?

It's easy to say we love something. We say we LOVE pizza and LOVE video games. But real love is an ACTION. We know someone loves us when they do something nice or kind.

- How does God SHOW He loves us? *(He sent His Son, Jesus. He made us and everything else. He helps us, etc.)*
- How can someone YOUR age show love to people?

GOD SHOWS LOVE, SO I CAN LOVE OTHERS.

ACTIVITY 3: LOVELY SCAVENGER HUNT

MATERIALS: Pictures of different objects that could be used to show love like food, lawn mower, letters, etc. Anything that could be used to show someone you care will work fine. (one picture for each child)

DIRECTIONS: Hide pictures of these different objects around the room. Give kids a chance to find all the pictures. Then let kids get into groups of four or five, and brainstorm ways they could use the objects in the pictures to show Jesus' love to other people. After a little while, let kids switch objects with someone in a different group, then brainstorm about that object with their group.

ACTIVITY OPTION:

Bring real objects rather than pictures of objects to hide around the room. Being able to hold the object might help some kids make the connection.

CAMPFIRE CONNECTION:

Gather everyone back into a large group, and allow a few kids to share their ideas.

Sometimes it's hard to think of a way to show God's love to others. You can ask God to open your eyes and your heart to things around you that can help you show others God's love. After all, God shows us His love in so many ways! He allowed Peter to heal the crippled man and tell others how much God loved them. He invites us to be a part of His family, provides for us, and takes care of us – the list goes on and on! We can show others the kind of love God shows us just like Peter did.

ACTIVITY 4: CHARADES

MATERIALS: None

DIRECTIONS: Whisper the name of an animal to someone, so only they can hear. The child tries to act out the animal without using any sound effects or words. The first person to guess the animal wins and gets to act out the next animal for the class.

CAMPFIRE CONNECTION:

It's hard sometimes to communicate without words. Words are important, but they don't mean much if we don't back up our words with our actions.

- How can we act out God's love to others?

MEMORY VERSE: GALATIANS 5:22-23

MATERIALS: “Fruit of the Spirit” song (several versions of this song can be found online via YouTube and other streaming services), Music player

DIRECTIONS: Write the memory verse on the board for everyone to see. Read the verse together. Play the song for your class. Teach fun motions to go with each fruit, or let your class make up their own fun motions.

CAMPFIRE CONNECTION:

When a tree is healthy, it gives off fruit. Apple trees give apples, pear trees give pears, and pine trees give pine cones. What does a healthy and growing Christian give? *(The fruit of the Spirit of God!)* As we grow in our friendship with God, we begin to become more like Him.

Today we learned the many ways God’s love rubs off on us.

- How does God show His love for us?
- How can we show God’s love to others?

“But the fruit of the Spirit is love, joy, peace, patience, kindness, goodness, faithfulness, gentleness, self control; against such things there is no law.”

GALATIANS 5:22-23

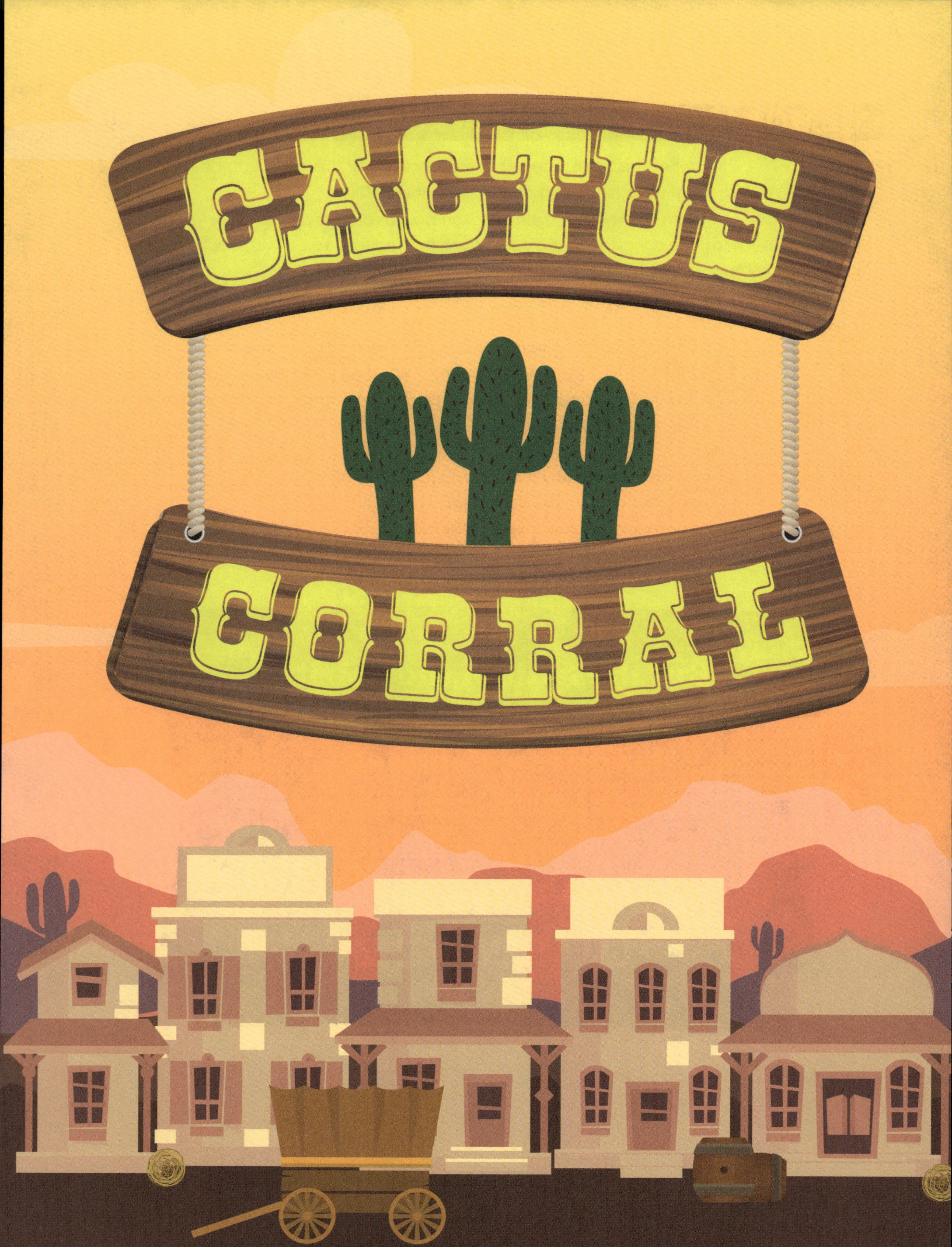
CACTUS
CORRAL

LESSON 2

MAIN POINT

God Brings Joy,
so I Can Be Joyful.

BIBLE STORY

Paul and Silas Sing in Prison.
(Acts 16:16-40)

MEMORY VERSE

"But the fruit of the Spirit is love, joy, peace, patience, kindness, goodness, faithfulness, gentleness, self control; against such things there is no law." Galatians 5:22-23 [NASB]

DON'T BE A PRICKLY PEAR!

SUPPLIES FROM THE GENERAL STORE

Activity 1:
None

Activity 2:
Chairs or Masking tape

Bible Lesson:
Fruit of the Spirit poster (See page 5) and Joy sticker

Activity 3:
Rope or yarn, Small balloons

Activity 4:
None

Activity 5:
Masking or Velcro tape

Memory Verse:
"Fruit of the Spirit" song (several versions of this song can be found online via YouTube and other streaming services), Music player

LEADER DEVOTION

READ

Acts 16:16-40

Had Paul and Silas been ordinary men, they would have despaired when they were wrongfully beaten and imprisoned. They would have rejoiced at the opportunity to escape. They were not ordinary men though, because they had a relationship with the one true God. Their relationship with God gave them the power to have unwavering joy even in ever-changing circumstances.

Paul and Silas placed their measure of success, self-worth, sense of purpose, and happiness in God. They were confident in His care; therefore, they were able to sing and speak of Him even while wearing chains in the darkness of the inner prison. And even from the depths of the inner prison, God heard their worship. There is no place on earth, no circumstance, in which we cannot rejoice in God. Because they were confident of Christ's care for them, they were able to care for the jailer when the opportunity for escape came.

Today it might seem odd the jailer would have opted to commit suicide at the thought of losing so many prisoners. At that time, Roman guards who lost their prisoners were sentenced to die in the same shameful manner their lost prisoners would have, had they not escaped. In addition, the cultural importance of duty and honor was very high in Rome. The jailer's suicide would have been seen as an honorable death. Instead, Paul and Silas chose not to leave. Imagine the jailer's confusion listening to the songs from the inner prison, then seeing the men stay when they easily could have escaped. Paul and Silas shared Christ with the jailer and his family, and he rejoiced!

Sharing Christ is sharing joy. Unlike happiness, joy is not based on circumstances. True joy comes from having a relationship with our unchanging God. In **Philippians 4:4** Paul says to a persecuted church, **"Always be full of joy in the Lord. I say it again—rejoice!"** In Christ, we have many reasons to rejoice. Take time to list out the reasons we have to be joyful. Then, prayerfully consider the things that attempt to steal your joy. Like Paul and Silas, resolve with the Lord to rejoice always and in every circumstance. As Nehemiah said in **Nehemiah 8:10, "the joy of the Lord is your strength!"**

WELCOME

ACTIVITY 1: THE LAUGHING GAME

MATERIALS: None

DIRECTIONS: Get a partner and take turns making funny faces at each other. The first to laugh loses.

CAMPFIRE CONNECTION:

- Was it fun to laugh with your friends?
- Do you always feel like laughing?
- When are some times you wouldn't feel like laughing?

Our Bible lesson today is all about JOY. Joy is different from being happy. Sometimes bad things happen, and we don't feel very happy. Happiness comes from our situation, but joy comes from God. JOY is something we can have no matter what happens!

NOTE

Kids pick up on everything you do. If you are having fun and showing JOY, so will they! Remember to have joy no matter what happens today. Your example is the most powerful lesson you will have the opportunity to teach.

ACTIVITY OPTIONS:

Bring some good, clean joke books for kids to look through.

. . . .

Decorate your room in bright colors for a party today. Celebrate everything that God has done to bring us joy.

. . . .

Teach your kids a cheer about JOY:
"J is for JESUS
O is for OTHERS
Y-Y-Y-Y-Y-Y is for
YOU - YOU - YOU! "

ACTIVITY 2: BALLOON VOLLEYBALL

MATERIALS: Chairs or Masking tape

DIRECTIONS: Set up chairs (or put tape on the floor) across the room to serve as a volleyball net. Throw out a balloon as the volleyball and let kids hit it back and forth. If the balloon touches the ground on Team 1's side, Team 2 gets a point, and vice versa. If you have a lot of kids playing, you may want to add some balloons to ensure everyone gets to participate.

CAMPFIRE CONNECTION:

- Would this game have been as fun if we had decided to play with a fifty pound weight instead of a balloon? Why not? *(It would be too heavy, someone might get hurt.)*
- What makes a balloon fun to play with in this game? *(It's light.)*

The balloon is filled with air, so it floats and is fun to play with. In the same way, when we are filled with God's joy, our lives are much more fun than if we were filled with the heavy weight of our sin.

GOD BRINGS JOY, SO I CAN BE JOYFUL.

BIBLE LESSON

GOD BRINGS JOY, SO I CAN BE JOYFUL.

INTRO

In Galatians 5:22-23, Paul talks about some of the ways knowing God shows up in our lives. He calls these things the fruit of the Spirit. For the next few weeks, we are going to learn about the fruit of the Spirit by studying some of the first Christians, the first people to have the Holy Spirit living inside of them. Today we are going to learn about the ways that God's joy rubs off on us.

JOY

STICKER STOP

Place the Joy Sticker on your Fruit of the Spirit poster *(See page 5).*

The kind of joy we are learning about today is different from happiness.

- When do you feel happy? *(birthday parties, playing with friends, Christmas morning, etc.)*

Most people feel happy when good things happen and feel sad when bad things happen. Joy is a kind of happiness that Christians have when either good or bad things happen. Lots of things can keep you from being happy, but if you have Jesus in your life, nothing can take away your JOY. When bad things happen or you just have a bad day, remember to ask Jesus to give you joy. Choose to have an attitude that shows others how amazing Jesus is no matter what.

Today we are going to learn about two people in Acts who were in a very bad situation. Even though bad things happened, they still had joy, the second fruit of the Spirit listed in Galatians 5.

READ THE BIBLE

Open your Bibles to Acts 16. Acts is a history book about the early church after Jesus ascended (went up) back to Heaven. It is in the New Testament.

At this time, Paul and Silas were traveling around the world, and telling people the Good News about Jesus. One day, they met a woman who was possessed. The spirit in her could tell the future, and evil men were using her to make money instead of trying to help her. Because Paul knew Jesus, he told the evil spirit to leave the woman in Jesus' name. This was great news for the woman, but the evil men were very angry. They had Paul and Silas beaten and thrown into the inner prison, even though they had not done anything wrong. The inner prison is a very dark part of the prison, where people were chained to the walls and floors.

- How would you feel if you were Paul or Silas?
- Do you think they were happy?
- Do you think they had joy?

Paul and Silas were not having a very good day!

Read Acts 16:25.

Paul and Silas were singing praises to God! Everyone in the prison could hear them sing worship songs to God. Of course, Paul and Silas were not happy about being in prison, but they were happy they knew Jesus. Knowing Jesus is always a reason to celebrate, and they wanted to tell everyone about Him. While they were singing, something amazing happened.

Read Acts 16:26-30.

Paul and Silas could have escaped, but they chose to stay. The Roman jailer would have gotten into a lot of trouble if everyone had escaped on his watch. Paul and Silas told the jailer about Jesus.

PRESENT THE GOSPEL

Acts 16:31 says, "...Believe in the Lord Jesus, and you will be saved...". What did the jailer need to be saved from? The punishment for his sins. Like you and me, the jailer had chosen to do things his way instead of God's way. He had chosen to do wrong.

The punishment for sin is death and separation from God. Jesus, God's perfect Son, came to take our punishment for us. He died on the cross even though He had not done anything wrong. Then Jesus came back to life three days later! Now we can have a friendship with God, and nothing can take that friendship away from us. Admit you have sinned, that you have chosen to do wrong. Tell God you believe in Him, that He died and came back to life for you. Thank Him for all He has done for you. Then choose to put Jesus in charge of your life. Make Him the Lord, the Boss, of your life from now on.

READ THE BIBLE

When Paul and Silas told the jailer and his family about Jesus, they believed right away. They were then baptized to show they would never be the same again.

Read Acts 16:34.

The jailer and his family rejoiced! They had joy now, too, because they knew Jesus.

APPLICATION

No matter what happens, the fact that Jesus loves you will always be true. That is something to be joyful about. No matter what happens, the fact that Jesus wants you to be His friend will always be true. That is amazing! So the next time you feel sad, remember Jesus brings joy. It is okay to be sad when sad things happen, but we should remember Jesus will always be there. He is the reason to be joyful.

PRAY

Let's take time right now to praise God for all of the amazing reasons He has given us to be joyful.

Give kids an opportunity to thank God in prayer for what He has done.

ACTIVITY 3: ALL TIED UP

MATERIALS: Rope or yarn, Small balloons

DIRECTIONS: Split your class into even numbered teams. Have kids pair up within their teams and tie their legs together for a three-legged race. Set balloons on one side of the room and have teams line up on the opposite side. Teams run in a relay to grab a small balloon. The first team to put all their balloons in a straight line and sit down wins!

CAMPFIRE CONNECTION:

- Was it hard to do the relay when you were tied up?
- How did it feel to be tied up?

Our Bible lesson today is all about two men who were all tied up in prison. But even though Paul and Silas were in prison, these men still had JOY! Sometimes, we get tied down by our circumstances. We have a bad day or someone says something that hurts our feelings. But no matter what happens around us, we know we can have God's JOY!

ACTIVITY OPTION:

To add difficulty, ask kids to draw pictures with their wrists tied to a partner's wrist.

. . . .

For added fun, have kids sing a song while running the relay race just like Paul and Silas sang in prison.

ACTIVITY 4: MUSH

MATERIALS: None

DIRECTIONS: Have kids stand in a circle. One child stands in the middle and points to someone. That person must say "Mush" and then stay perfectly still and quiet, while the person in the middle tries to make them laugh. If they don't laugh after a few seconds, the center person has to pick someone else. That person must say "Mush Mush." If they still don't laugh, the third person picked must say, " Mush Mush Mush" and so on. When someone laughs, they become the new center person.

CAMPFIRE CONNECTION:

Sometimes, life feels great: everything is all smiles and laughs. Other times though, life feels like MUSH. But because God brings JOY, we can have JOY, even when life feels like mush!

ACTIVITY 5: JAIL TAG

MATERIALS: Masking or Velcro tape

DIRECTIONS: Mark off a box in the middle of the room to be "jail." Choose one person to be the jailer and two people to be "earthquakes." Everyone else is a missionary. The jailer tries to tag the missionaries. When tagged, missionaries must go to jail until an earthquake gently shakes them, and they are free. Play a few rounds so everyone gets to play a different role in each game.

ACTIVITY OPTION:

You may also choose to play this game like freeze tag. Instead of sending tagged missionaries to jail, have them freeze in place until an earthquake gently shakes them back into action.

CAMPFIRE CONNECTION:

- Missionaries – how did it feel to be put in jail? How did it feel to be freed by the earthquake?

Being in jail is no fun! The Roman government didn't want Paul and Silas to share the JOY of God with others. They tried to steal their joy by locking them up in maximum security, but Paul and Silas wouldn't let other people, or even a jail cell, steal their joy. Paul and Silas didn't like being in jail, but they knew that they would be okay no matter what happened. Their confidence in God brought them joy even in the middle of a stinky old jail cell.

- Jailers – How did it feel to see your prisoners set free by the earthquakes?

Back in Roman times, a guard would be killed if they let any prisoners escape! When the earthquake set Paul and Silas free, the jailer was afraid for his life. He was afraid he and his whole family would be put to shame, because he had lost the prisoners! Thankfully for the jailer, Paul and Silas stayed in jail even though they could have run away. The joy of the Lord was enough for them. Because of their joy, they were able to lead the jailer to Jesus and spread His JOY!!!

GOD BRINGS JOY, SO I CAN BE JOYFUL.

MEMORY VERSE: GALATIANS 5:22-23

MATERIALS: "Fruit of the Spirit" song (several versions of this song can be found online via YouTube and other streaming services), Music player

DIRECTIONS: Write the memory verse on the board for everyone to see. Read the verse together. Play the song for your class. Teach fun motions to go with each characteristic of the fruit or let your class make up their own fun motions.

CAMPFIRE CONNECTION:

When a tree is healthy, it gives off fruit. Apple trees give apples, pear trees give pears, and pine trees give pine cones. What does a healthy and growing Christian give? *(The fruit of the Spirit of God!)* As we grow in our friendship with God, we begin to become more like Him.

Today we learned about the many ways God's joy rubs off on us.

- What is the difference between happiness and joy?
- How can we have joy on good days and bad days?

> **"But the fruit of the Spirit is love, joy, peace, patience, kindness, goodness, faithfulness, gentleness, self control; against such things there is no law."**
>
> **GALATIANS 5:22-23**

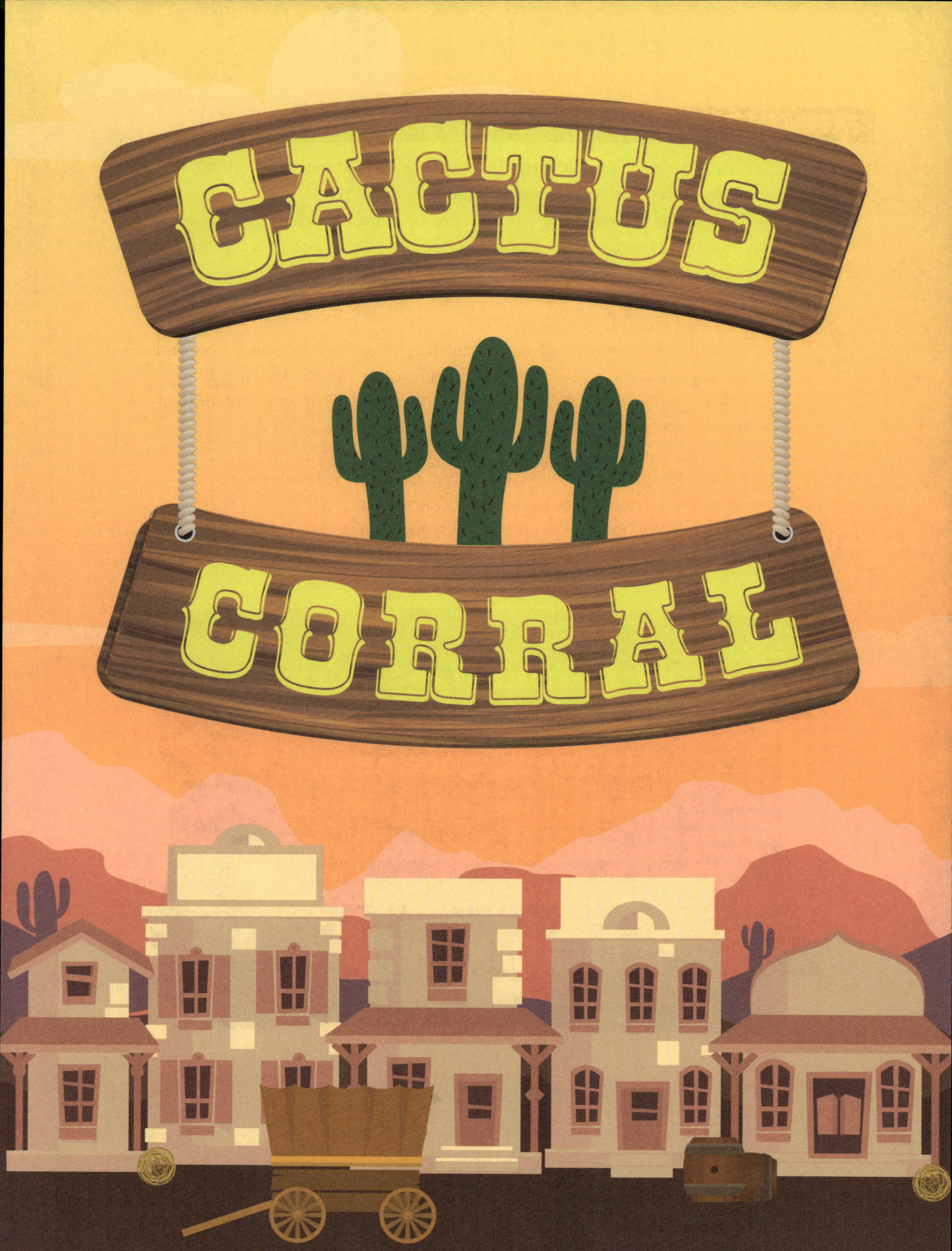
CACTUS
CORRAL

LESSON 3

MAIN POINT

God Brings Peace,
so I Can Be Peaceful.

BIBLE STORY

Paul Makes Peace with God.
(Acts 9:1-31)

MEMORY VERSE

"But the fruit of the Spirit is love, joy, peace, patience, kindness, goodness, faithfulness, gentleness, self control; against such things there is no law." Galatians 5:22-23 [NASB]

DON'T BE A PRICKLY PEAR!

SUPPLIES FROM THE

GENERAL STORE

Activity 1:

None

Activity 2:

Toilet paper, Tin foil, Masking tape,
Other "decorating" supplies

Bible Lesson:

Fruit of the Spirit poster (See page 5) and Peace sticker

Activity 3:

Balloons

Activity 4:

Bed sheet or sheets of butcher paper taped together,
Beach balls

Memory Verse:

"Fruit of the Spirit" song (several versions of this song can be found online via YouTube and other streaming services), Music player

LEADER DEVOTION

READ

Acts 9:1-31

Everyone wants peace. Many work towards peace internally, focusing on the things they must personally change. "If I could only achieve or have or become *this*, everything would be right." Some work towards peace externally, focusing on the things others need to change. "If *they* would only ______, everything would be right." While this may bring a temporary perception of peace, neither of these tactics will bring true, lasting peace.

Saul, a respected leader of the Pharisees, also sought peace. The Followers of The Way (Christ followers) were causing trouble for Pharisees who refused to recognize Jesus as the Messiah. Saul, an extreme rule-follower, decided to take action against the troublemakers, in order to achieve peace for the Pharisees. He was so consumed by his mission that he did not realize his fight was actually against the Prince of Peace. Then, while he was on his way to wage more war against followers of Jesus, Peace found Saul.

From that moment on, Saul's life changed dramatically. Falling from his high position with the Pharisees, Saul began a new life preaching Christ all over the world. He was beaten and imprisoned numerous times, finally giving his life rather than denying Christ. From a superficial view, Saul's life seems to have gone from relative peace to absolute chaos. However in Christ, the opposite is true. Saul gave up a life of false peace and war with God to gain a life of absolute peace and friendship with God. Everything about Saul changed that day on the road to Damascus, because Jesus, the Prince of Peace, found him.

In John 14:27 Jesus says, "I am leaving you with a gift – peace of mind and heart. And the peace I give is a gift the world cannot give. So don't be troubled or afraid."

Philippians 4:6-7 says, "Don't worry about anything; instead, pray about everything. Tell God what you need, and thank him for all he has done. Then you will experience God's peace, which exceeds anything we can understand. His peace will guard your hearts and minds as you live in Christ Jesus."

God's peace cannot be earned or achieved: It is freely given! Resolve to stop striving for peace, and freely share His peace instead. Let His peace govern your heart and mind, even in the midst of chaos.

WELCOME

ACTIVITY 1: ON THE ROAD AGAIN

MATERIALS: None

DIRECTIONS: Have kids sit in a circle. Tell them to be thinking of an object that could represent a talent they have or something they like to do. The first person says, "My name is (Kelly), and I'm on the road again. I brought an (mp3 player)." The next person in the circle says, "My name is (Amy), and I'm on the road again. I brought an mp3 player and a (movie)." Kids go around the circle, adding items to the list each time. See how many things your kids can remember. You can also give bonus points to kids who can remember everyone's name in the class.

CAMPFIRE CONNECTION:

Our Bible story today is about someone who was "on the road again." Saul was not a very nice man. He was at war with God. He traveled around to find Christians and kill them! Then on the road to Damascus, Saul met the Prince of Peace, Jesus! Through Jesus, God made peace with Saul.

Like Saul, we have all sinned, made wrong choices that take us away from God. God wants to give us His peace through a relationship with His Son, Jesus.

GOD BRINGS PEACE, SO I CAN BE PEACEFUL.

ACTIVITY 2: BEST IN SHOW

MATERIALS: Toilet paper, Tin foil, Masking tape, Other "decorating" supplies
DIRECTIONS: Split your class into 4 or 5 smaller groups. Hand out supplies to each group and instruct them to decorate one person in the group as a horse. Everyone must participate in order for your horse to win Best in Show! After a while, have a horse show and hand out awards! (The awards can be as simple as blue ribbons made from paper.)

CAMPFIRE CONNECTION:

- What kind of things did you put on your friends to make them look like a horse?
- If you had a little more time and maybe some more supplies, do you think you could have made your friends look even MORE like a horse?
- Would you ever be able to turn them into a horse?

Of course not! You could make your person look a lot LIKE a real horse, but they would never BE an actual horse!! In the same way, we can try very hard to create peace in our lives. Some people work very hard trying to make this happen. They think if they can do, be, or have certain things that their lives will be better, more peaceful. But nothing WE can do will give us real peace – just like nothing you can do will turn you into a horse!

Jesus knew we couldn't have real peace on our own, so He came to save us and help us make peace with God. Jesus, the Prince of Peace, is the ONLY way to Heaven. Now we can choose to follow Him and accept His free gift of salvation and the peace of God.

BIBLE LESSON

GOD BRINGS PEACE, SO I CAN BE PEACEFUL.

INTRO

In Galatians 5:22-23, Paul talks about some of the ways knowing God shows up in our lives. He calls these things the fruit of the Spirit. For the next few weeks, we are going to learn about the fruit of the Spirit by studying some of the first Christians, the first people to have the Holy Spirit living inside of them. Today we are going to learn about the ways that God gives us peace.

STICKER STOP

Place the Peace Sticker on your Fruit of the Spirit poster *(See page 5).*

What is peace? Peace is one of those words that can probably best be understood by what it is not. What is NOT peace?

The peace we are talking about today is different from a quiet moment. God's peace is not being worried or afraid. The tie-dye on the sticker has a lot of crazy colors, doesn't it? Sometimes life can be a little crazy, but we know Jesus came to give us His PEACE! No matter what goes on in our lives, we know Jesus will bring us peace: peace with God AND peace in everyday life.

God's peace comes from being able to completely trust God for everything. Everyone wants to have peace in life. Some people try to make peace happen for themselves. They believe if they had enough money, they wouldn't need to worry. Other people think if they find a best friend, husband, or wife they will feel at peace. But the truth is, no one can find peace apart from God. God's peace is a free gift He gives us through a relationship with His Son, Jesus.

READ THE BIBLE

Open your Bibles to Acts 9. Acts is a book of the Bible in the New Testament about the history of the first Christians. At first, people who believed in Jesus were called "Followers of The Way." Peter and the other apostles were preaching about Jesus, and more and more people came to believe in Jesus as their Lord and Savior.

But not everyone believed Jesus was God's Son. Saul, a respected Pharisee leader, did not believe Jesus was God's Son. In fact, Saul did not want anyone to talk about Jesus. The Pharisees gave Saul permission to find and kill anyone who believed in Jesus. Saul thought he was doing something that would bring peace for himself and the rest of the Pharisees. He did not understand that Jesus really was God's Son. While Saul was on the way to Damascus to find people who believed in Jesus, something amazing happened that changed Saul's life and brought him real peace.

Read Acts 9:1-9.

Jesus appeared to Saul! Do you think Saul believed that Jesus was God's Son now? Yes, he did.

Meanwhile, the Lord spoke to a man named Ananias, who lived in Damascus. God told Ananias to go to Saul and heal his eyes, so he could see again. Ananias had heard about Saul and was afraid to speak to him, but he obeyed God. When Ananias had healed Saul's blindness, Saul was baptized and filled with the Holy Spirit. He finally understood Jesus was God!

PRESENT THE GOSPEL

Saul started on the road to Damascus on a mission to bring peace for himself and the Pharisees. Instead, Jesus, the Prince of Peace, brought peace to him. The Bible tells us in Romans 3:23 that every person has sinned. We have all chosen to do wrong. When we sin, it is like we are turning our backs on God. That is not good! The punishment we deserve for these wrong choices is death and separation from God. Thankfully, Jesus came to bring peace. There is nothing we can do to fix our broken relationship with God. Doing good things, having a good family, and even going to church is not enough to bring peace between us and God. It is not enough to get us to Heaven. Jesus came, lived a perfect life, and took the punishment we deserved, when He chose to die on the cross. Then three days later, Jesus came back to life! Now we can be at peace with God. We can have a friendship with Jesus! Admit you have sinned. Believe Jesus is

God's Son, who died and rose again. Choose to put Jesus in charge of your life from now on. Jesus came to bring us peace. It is a free gift from God. All we have to do is accept it.

READ THE BIBLE

After Saul met Jesus, his whole life changed. He started to tell people all over the world the Good News about Jesus. Saul eventually changed his name to Paul - the same Paul we learned about last week! Jesus gave Paul peace with God. Even though he was beaten and imprisoned for telling people about Jesus, Paul always had God's peace.

APPLICATION

God's peace is different from a quiet moment. God's peace is a gift of friendship that lasts. If you have not received God's gift of peace, if you have not made Jesus the Boss of your life, talk to us about it today. We would love to tell you more about Him.

If you have already made the decision to follow Christ, how do you show God's peace to others? Think about the way you treat your brothers and sisters. Do you try to start arguments with them or do things that you know will bother them? Or do you treat them the way Jesus would treat them? Think about the way you act when you are losing a game. Are you kind to others, enjoying the game, or do you let your anger get the best of you? Having a relationship with Jesus allows us to be peaceful in our relationships with others, no matter what is going on. Talk to Jesus about peace. Ask Him to help you show His peace to others, no matter what is going on around you.

PRAY

GOD BRINGS PEACE, SO I CAN BE PEACEFUL.

ACTIVITY 3: ON MY OWN RELAY

MATERIALS: Balloons

DIRECTIONS: Split your class into several teams. One at a time, kids try to carry a balloon on their back while crawling. Kids must go across the room and back without dropping the balloon. If they drop the balloon, they have to start over.

After trying to play this way for a while, stop the game and amend the rules. Now, kids pick a partner to carry the balloon for them while they crawl across the room and back. This version of the game will go much faster! When everyone on the team has gone, the team must pop their balloon and sit down. The first team to do this wins!

CAMPFIRE CONNECTION:

- Which version of the game was more fun? Why?
- What made the first version hard?
- Think of a time you needed help because you couldn't do it on your own. Would someone like to share a story about when they needed help?

The Bible says all of us need help. We can't get to Heaven on our own because we have sin in our lives. Sin is any choice we make that would hurt the heart of God. Everyone has sinned, or done something they know is wrong (Romans 3:23). Just like no one could get all the way across the room and back with the balloon on their back, no one can get to Heaven with sin, because Heaven is a perfect place. Our sin makes us at war with God. Jesus came, because He knew we needed help. Jesus came to take our sins away, so that we could be at peace with God. He came to forgive us for the wrong things we have done, so we could go to Heaven one day and be with Him forever. No one can earn Heaven on their own. But if we choose to follow Him, Jesus will give us the free gift of forgiveness for our sins, forever friendship with God, and a forever home in Heaven!

ACTIVITY 4: HUMAN BATTLESHIP

MATERIALS: Bed sheet or sheets of butcher paper taped together, Beach balls

DIRECTIONS: Split your class into 2 teams. Hold up a sheet between the two teams as a net, or drape the sheet over a line of chairs. Teams should not be able to see each other. Kids must lie on their backs. Once the game starts, they can't move! Throw out a few beach balls. Kids throw the balls over the net to try to "sink" someone on the other side. If someone is hit by a ball, (remember: kids can't move to dodge them), they are out and become a General. Generals may tell their teammates where to aim their next throws to sink the other team. The first team to completely sink the other team wins!

ACTIVITY OPTION:

Add rules as you go to make the game more fun. For example, you may add that catching a ball makes you safe or that kids can only move twice during the game.

CAMPFIRE CONNECTION:

That was a fun game! Unfortunately, being at war for real is not fun.

- Have you ever had an argument with someone you love? (Maybe a parent or friend)
- How did it feel to be "at war" with them?
- What do you think it means to be "at war" with God?

When we choose to sin, the Bible says we are choosing to be God's enemy. (James 4:4, Romans 5:10) God loves us SO much! It hurts Him when we choose to be at war with Him by sinning.
After the argument you talked about earlier, did you make it right? In other words, how did you make peace with that person?
How did God make peace with us?

Romans 5:1 says, "Therefore, since we have been made right in God's sight by faith, we have peace with God because of what Jesus Christ our Lord has done for us."

Romans 5:10 says, "For since our friendship with God was restored by the death of his Son while we were still his enemies, we will certainly be saved through the life of his Son."

Jesus came to take the punishment for our sins so we could be at peace with God! We deserve to be at war, but Jesus came to bring PEACE. We now can choose to accept Jesus' gift of peace.

MEMORY VERSE: GALATIANS 5:22-23

MATERIALS: "Fruit of the Spirit" song (several versions of this song can be found online via YouTube and other streaming services), Music player

DIRECTIONS: Write the memory verse on the board for everyone to see. Read the verse together. Play the song for your class. Teach fun motions to go with each characteristic of the fruit or let your class make up their own fun motions.

CAMPFIRE CONNECTION:

When a tree is healthy, it gives off fruit. Apple trees give apples, pear trees give pears, and pine trees give pine cones. What does a healthy and growing Christian give? *(The fruit of the Spirit of God!)* As we grow in our friendship with God, we begin to become more like Him.

Today we learned about the ways that God's peace rubs off on us.

- How does God bring peace to us?
- What is the difference between someone who has God's peace and someone who does not?

"But the fruit of the Spirit is love, joy, peace, patience, kindness, goodness, faithfulness, gentleness, self control; against such things there is no law."

GALATIANS 5:22-23

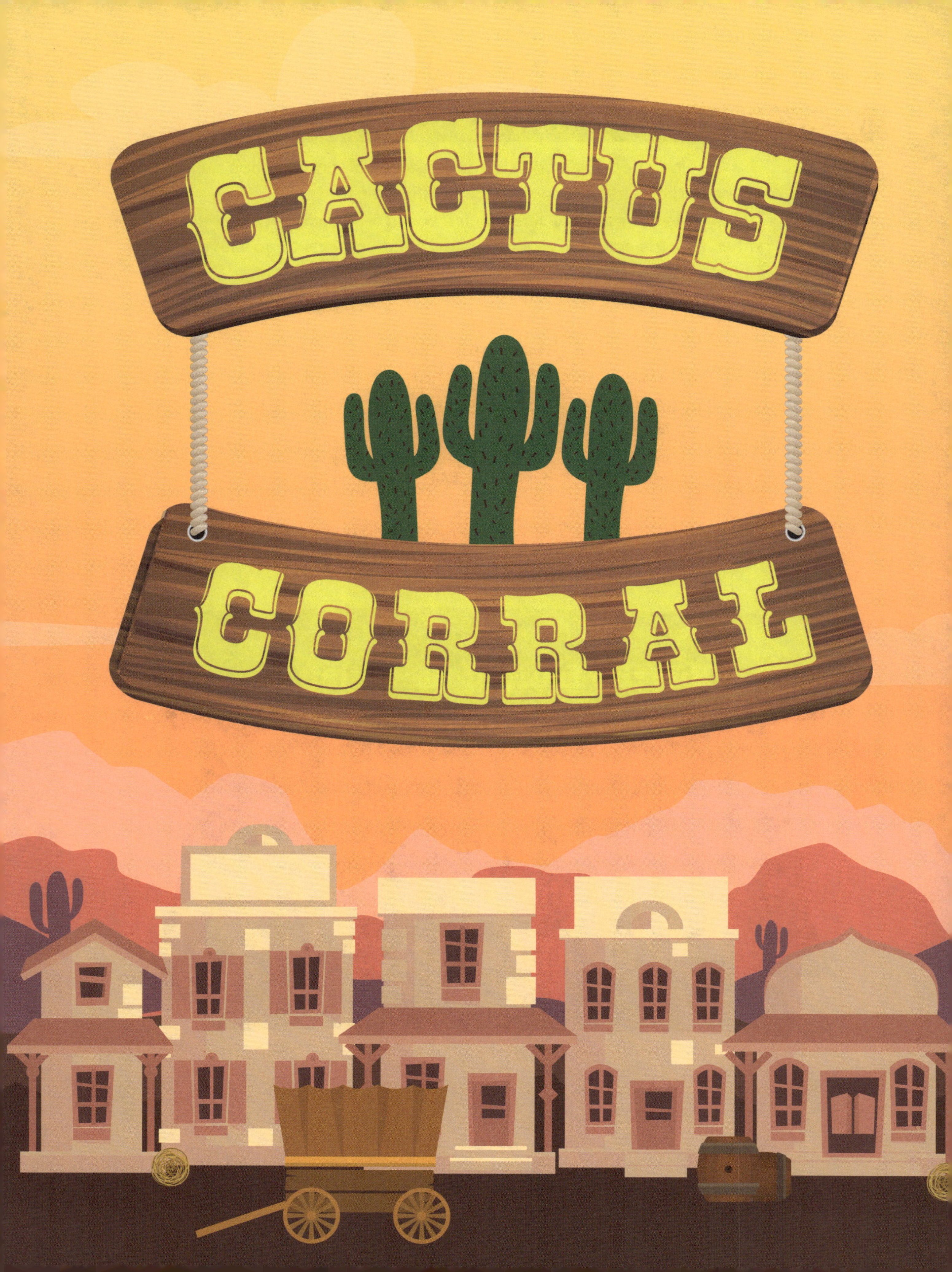
CACTUS
CORRAL

LESSON 4

MAIN POINT

God Shows Patience, so I Can Be Patient.

BIBLE STORY

Paul Is Shipwrecked. (Acts 27)

MEMORY VERSE

"But the fruit of the Spirit is love, joy, peace, patience, kindness, goodness, faithfulness, gentleness, self control; against such things there is no law." Galatians 5:22-23 [NASB]

DON'T BE A PRICKLY PEAR!

SUPPLIES FROM THE GENERAL STORE

Activity 1:

Dominoes, Cards, Block stacking game,
Art supplies, Paper,
Dot painting, Pick up sticks

Bible Lesson:

Fruit of the Spirit poster (See page 5) and Patience sticker

Activity 2:

None

Activity 3:

Spoons for each child, Ping pong balls

Memory Verse:

"Fruit of the Spirit" song (several versions of this song can be found online via YouTube and other streaming services), Music player

LEADER DEVOTION

READ

Acts 27

Paul had once again been accused by the Jews, his own people, for preaching the Good News of Jesus, a crime for which a Roman citizen should not have been imprisoned. When the centurion heard of a plot to kill Paul, he ordered Paul to be brought before Felix. Two years after Paul had been sentenced to house arrest pending further investigation, the Jews once again brought up serious and unproven charges against him in an attempt on his life. Rather than be tried by the Jews, Paul appealed to Caesar. In each court appearance, Paul used his trial as an opportunity to tell the Truth of Jesus' resurrection. In Acts 27, Paul was on his way to Rome to stand trial before Caesar.

If anyone has ever had a good reason to give in to fear and impatience, it was Paul. After ignoring Paul's advice, everyone on the ship was in danger of losing their lives to the great storm. Going days and days without food, the crew began to lose hope. Paul, by the world's standards, had every right to abandon them and attempt to save himself. Instead, he encouraged his captors and communicated God's message of hope to everyone on board. They would all survive the storm. After suffering the consequences of ignoring Paul's advice the first time, the centurion was determined not to make the same mistake twice. He cut away the life rafts from the ship and kept the soldiers from murdering the prisoners. Every person reached shore alive, as the Lord had told Paul.

Imagine being an innocent prisoner on that boat, ignored and tossed back and forth by the waves, going without food for weeks on end. How patient would you be with your captors? How patient would you be in Paul's situation? But Paul knew God is in control of everything, including time. While he waited under house arrest and dealt with difficult people, Paul chose to focus on His Lord and Savior, Jesus Christ. He used every opportunity to spread the Good News. Paul's patience with his captors and situation served as an incredible witness.

What about you? How patient are you with the difficult people God has placed in your life? Like Paul, do you use each opportunity to share the love of Christ, remembering His patience with you? Perhaps you are in a waiting period. Be encouraged that God is in control of the timeline of your life. Use this time of waiting to prepare for the things God has planned for you. Get to know Him more, and take hold of every opportunity to live for Him, as you wait patiently for His timing and His perfect plan for your life.

WELCOME

ACTIVITY 1: PATIENCE CENTERS

MATERIALS: Dominoes, Cards, Block stacking game, Art supplies, Paper, Dot painting, Pick up sticks

DIRECTIONS: Set up 5 stations around the room. Monitor as kids move from one activity to the next.

STATION 1: DOMINO CHAIN REACTION

Have kids set up a domino chain. Measure the chain to see who can make the longest chain or the chain with the most dominoes in it. Then let kids tip over a domino to start the chain reaction.

STATION 2: CARD HOUSE

See who can make the tallest card house or the house using the most cards.

STATION 3: BLOCK STACKING

At this station, kids can either just play the game or see how tall they can build the blocks before they fall over.

STATION 4: DOT PAINTING

Kids create a picture one dot at a time – no solid lines. Show kids an example of a dot painting, so they understand the big picture of what they are trying to do. You may want to give them a list of some objects to draw to help them get started.

STATION 5: PICK UP STICKS

Dump a bunch of sticks in a messy pile on the floor. Kids try to pick up one stick at a time without moving any of the other sticks. If they successfully get a single stick out of the pile without moving anything else, they get to keep the stick and try for another one. If they move another stick, though, their turn is over, and the next person gets to try to pick up a stick. The person with the most sticks at the end of the game wins.

CAMPFIRE CONNECTION:

- Were any of these activities hard? Why / why not?
- Was it important to have patience when doing any of these activities? Why?
- What happened when you were impatient? (dominoes fell, things fell apart)

To build the tallest tower or card house, win the most sticks, or make the best dot painting, you had to be very PATIENT! In the same way, we "win" when we are patient with the people around us.

- Have you ever had to wait for something? Tell us about it.
- Has anyone ever had to wait for you? Tell us about that, too.

At some point, we have all had to wait for someone or something. It's not always easy, but it is important that we show PATIENCE with others.

- What happens when we are impatient with people?
- Does it ever help to be impatient?

Of course not! Most of the time, it makes the situation worse! Just like our falling dominoes, card houses, and towers, impatience can have devastating results.

GOD SHOWS PATIENCE, SO I CAN BE PATIENT.

BIBLE LESSON

GOD SHOWS PATIENCE, SO I CAN BE PATIENT.

INTRO

In Galatians 5:22-23, Paul talks about some of the ways knowing God shows up in our lives. He calls these things the fruit of the Spirit. We are learning about the fruit of the Spirit by studying some of the first Christians, the first people to have the Holy Spirit living inside of them. Today we are going to learn about the ways God gives us patience.

STICKER STOP

Place the Patience Sticker on your Fruit of the Spirit poster *(See page 5).*

Who likes to wait in line? Who likes to wait your turn to play your favorite game? Nobody? Who likes to be patient with your younger brother or sister? We do not like to wait, do we? Being patient is hard, but patience is about more than just waiting nicely. Being patient also has to do with the way we treat people who are not nice to us or who just drive us crazy.

The clock on the patience sticker helps us remember that sometimes it's better to wait. Before getting angry with a friend or family member, look at your watch and remember, Jesus wants us to be patient with others. In today's Bible story, Paul had to wait for a long time to get out of jail. He also had to deal with some very difficult people. Listen for the many ways Paul showed this fruit of the Spirit, patience, in today's story.

READ THE BIBLE

The book of Acts tells us that Paul traveled all over the world telling people the Good News about Jesus. He knew Jesus as his Friend, his Savior, and his Boss and wanted everyone to have a relationship with God, too. Many of the Jews did not understand

Jesus really was God's Son. They hated it when Paul told people the Good News about Jesus, that Jesus was alive. A group of these Jews came together trying to kill Paul. They threw him into prison and made up charges against him. They wanted Paul to get the death penalty.

Paul spent a lot of time in jail and went before many different leaders to stand trial. Instead of being mean or hateful to the people who threw him in prison, Paul simply told the truth. He told everyone in court the truth about Jesus. One of the leaders did not know what to do with Paul. The Roman governor decided to put him under house arrest. Paul spent two years under house arrest before his trial was brought up again. Two years!

After two years, a new governor looked at Paul's case. The Jews brought more charges against Paul, hoping he would get the death penalty this time. Once again, Paul used his trial as an opportunity to tell everyone the Good News about Jesus. The new governor suggested that Paul should be tried by the Jews, since they were the ones who had a problem with him. But Paul appealed to Caesar rather than be tried by the Jews who obviously wanted to kill him. So Paul was sent on a ship to Rome to go to court before Caesar.

Open your Bibles to Acts 27. Paul had been on many ships in his lifetime, as he traveled the world telling everyone he could about the Good News of Jesus. Now on the way to Rome, Paul knew a storm was coming, but no one would listen to him.

Read Acts 27:9-11.

Paul knew bad weather was coming, but no one believed him.

- Have you ever had someone ignore you when you were trying to tell them something important? How did that make you feel?

Being ignored probably did not make Paul very happy, but he was patient with his captor. Then Acts 27 tells us a big storm came. The crew of the ship were afraid of losing their lives.

Read Acts 27: 21-26.

Paul could have kept this great news to himself, but he chose to share it with the crew. Paul chose to be patient with the people who had ignored him. He told them God would take care of them. After a long time battling the storm, everyone made it to shore safely. Paul healed many of the people who lived on the island and told them about Jesus.

PRESENT THE GOSPEL

We all are a little like the crew on Paul's boat. They should have listened to Paul, but they chose to do their own thing instead. They ended up in a big storm, because they ignored Paul. Many times, we do the same thing with God. God has told us the best way to live, but we often choose to ignore Him and do our own thing instead. And like the crew, our sins, our choices to ignore God and do our own things, bring us nothing but trouble. The Bible says the punishment for sin is death and separation from God. But God loves us so much that He sent His only Son, Jesus, to take the punishment each of us deserves for our sins.

2 Peter 3:8-9 says, "But you must not forget this one thing, dear friends: A day is like a thousand years to the Lord, and a thousand years is like a day. The Lord isn't really being slow about his promise, as some people think. No, he is being patient for your sake. He does not want anyone to be destroyed, but wants everyone to repent."

One day, Jesus will come back. No one knows when He will come, but we do know He wants everyone to turn away from their sins and choose to put Him in charge. Knowing Jesus is the most important and incredible relationship we will ever have. Do you know Him? If not, talk to us before you leave. We would love to tell you more about Jesus.

APPLICATION

Paul was patient while he was waiting in jail. He did not whine or complain. Instead, He told people the Good News about Jesus. Paul was also patient with the people who ignored him on the boat. Instead of being mean to them, Paul chose to encourage the people, and tell them about Jesus.

Everyone has someone or something in their life that tests patience. Instead of whining or complaining, focus your heart on God and what He wants you to do while you wait. Instead of being mean to people who annoy you, remember God loves those people just as much as He loves you. Ask God to give you patience and help you to treat them the way He treats you.

PRAY

ACTIVITY 2: SHIPWRECK SURVIVORS

MATERIALS: None

DIRECTIONS: Designate one corner of the room as the Shipwreck and an opposite corner as the Island. Kids must swim from the Shipwreck to the Island shore for safety, but there's a catch. Everyone must reach the Island at the same time, or they will all drown. Assign kids different swimming strokes they must use to reach shore. (Ex. backstroke, crab walk, tip-toe, freestyle, butterfly stroke, belly crawl, etc.) If someone reaches the Island before the rest of the group, everyone drowns. Start the game over until everyone reaches the Island safely.

CAMPFIRE CONNECTION:

- How did you make sure everyone reached the island safely?
- There were lots of different strokes people used while swimming to safety. How did you work together with people using a different stroke than yours?
- Did you ever want to rush ahead of them and just get to the island yourself?

Working with others is not always easy. We have to be PATIENT with people in a lot of different situations. In our Bible story today, Paul had to be patient with his fellow shipwrecked passengers. Paul could have yelled at them for not listening to him when he told them they would be shipwrecked. Instead, he patiently helped everyone to shore and even told them about Jesus!

- How can you show patience to your friends? Brothers and sisters? Parents? Teachers?
- How does God show patience with us?

God is patient with us when we continue to sin. If we ask God to forgive us, the Bible says He will! (1 John 1:9) He teaches us, day by day, to be more like Him. God doesn't expect us to all of a sudden be perfect. Of course, our life changes when we start to follow Jesus. Every day as we seek Him, we become a little more like Jesus – it's not an overnight thing. Because God shows patience with us, we should have patience with people around us.

ACTIVITY 3: SLOW AND STEADY

MATERIALS: Spoons for each child, Ping pong balls

DIRECTIONS: Split your group into teams for a relay race. Hand each child a spoon and each team one ping pong ball. One at a time, kids must carry a ping pong ball to the other side of the room and back. The ping pong ball must only touch the spoon that kids must hold in their mouths. No one can use their hands. If the ping pong ball is dropped at any time, the relay runner must start over. The first team to finish and sit down wins!

CAMPFIRE CONNECTION:

- Did anyone drop the ping pong ball because they were trying to go too fast?
- What was the easiest way to run this race?
- As the saying goes, "Slow and steady wins the race." What do you think that means? Give an example of showing patience.

Patience is not an easy thing to master. We like to be first in line. We don't really like to wait for anything.

- Is patience important to you? In other words, do you want people to be patient with you? Why / why not?
- Why do you think patience is important to God?

ACTIVITY OPTION:

ACT IT OUT
Let kids act out different situations that require patience.

. . . .

TALK IT OUT
Let kids share their stories about patience with a partner. This way, everyone gets to share a personal story.

GOD SHOWS PATIENCE, SO I CAN BE PATIENT.

MEMORY VERSE: GALATIANS 5:22-23

MATERIALS: "Fruit of the Spirit" song (several versions of this song can be found online via YouTube and other streaming services), Music player

DIRECTIONS: Write the memory verse on the board for everyone to see. Read the verse together. Play the song for your class. Teach fun motions to go with each characteristic of the fruit or let your class make up their own fun motions.

CAMPFIRE CONNECTION:

When a tree is healthy, it gives off fruit. Apple trees give apples, pear trees give pears, and pine trees give pine cones. What does a healthy and growing Christian give? *(The fruit of the Spirit of God!)* As we grow in our friendship with God, we begin to become more like Him.

Today we learned about the ways that God's patience rubs off on us.

- How does God show patience to us?
- What can we do when we begin to feel impatient?
- How can knowing God help us become more patient?

"But the fruit of the Spirit is love, joy, peace, patience, kindness, goodness, faithfulness, gentleness, self control; against such things there is no law."

GALATIANS 5:22-23

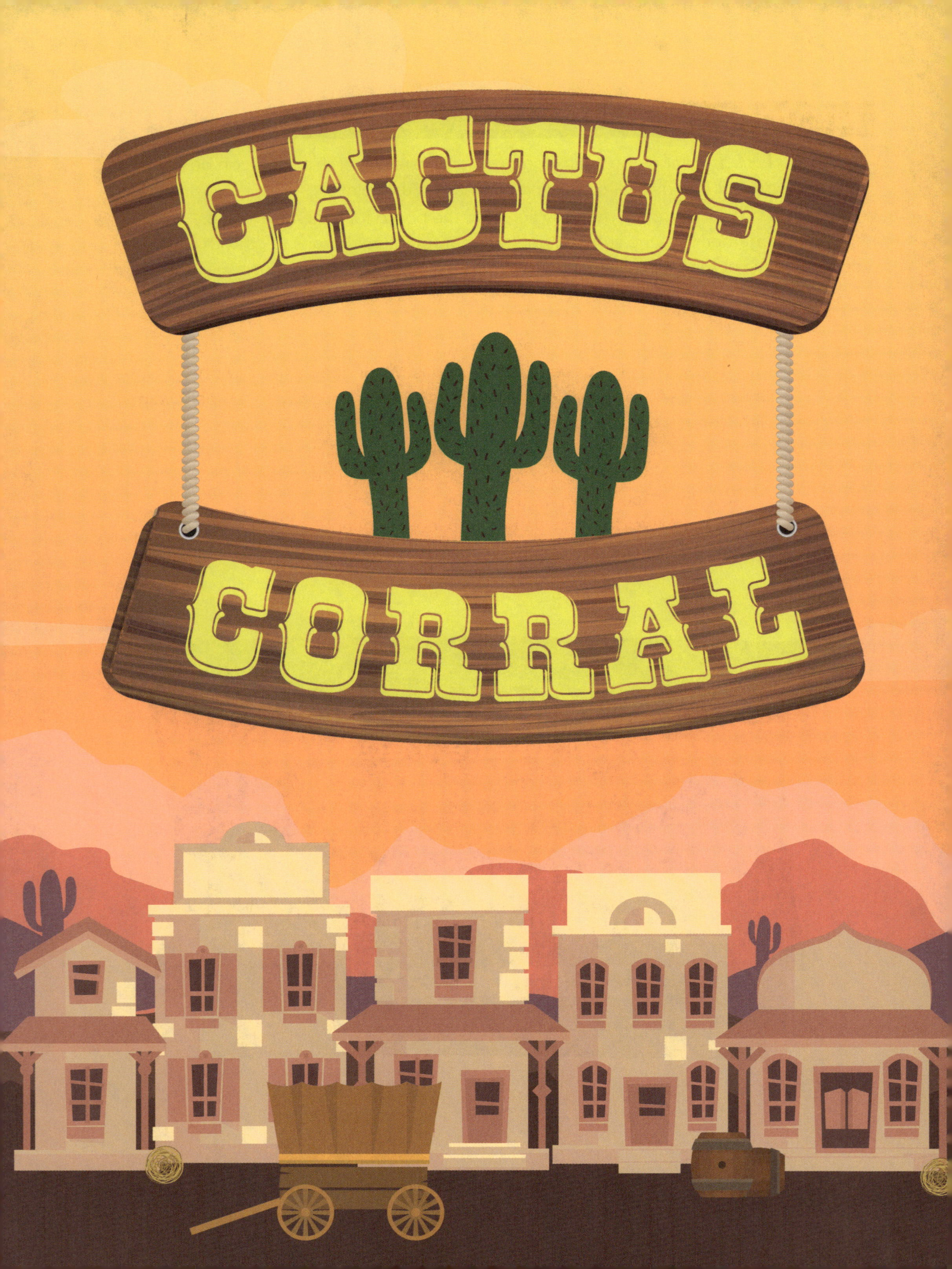
CACTUS
CORRAL

LESSON 5

MAIN POINT

God Shows Kindness,
so I Can Be Kind.

BIBLE STORY

Peter Tells Cornelius about Jesus.
(Acts 10)

MEMORY VERSE

"But the fruit of the Spirit is love, joy, peace, patience, kindness, goodness, faithfulness, gentleness, self control; against such things there is no law." Galatians 5:22-23 [NASB]

DON'T BE A PRICKLY PEAR!

SUPPLIES FROM THE GENERAL STORE

Activity 1:
Yardstick

Activity 2:
Different colored papers, Markers, Scissors,
White butcher paper

Bible Lesson:
Fruit of the Spirit poster (See page 5) and Kindness sticker

Activity 3:
Balloons

Activity 4:
None

Activity 5:
None

Memory Verse:
"Fruit of the Spirit" song (several versions of this song can be found online via YouTube and other streaming services), Music player

LEADER DEVOTION

READ

Acts 10

Throughout the Old Testament, God used the Jewish people to show Himself to the world. God made the Jews an object lesson of the Christian life and the vessel through which He would bring the promised Messiah. This is shown through Abraham's immediate family, the life of Joseph, Moses and the Exodus, the wilderness wanderings to reach the promised land, the law, the feasts, and more. Because God had previously dealt primarily with the Jews, Peter mistakenly thought that the Good News was meant only for the Jewish people and certainly not for the hated Roman soldiers. Through a vision, God expanded Peter's understanding of the Good News. Jesus died once for ALL, not just once for the Jews.

When Peter arrived at Cornelius' home, Cornelius was ready. He had gathered his friends and family to hear everything Peter had to say. Cornelius wanted to know more about God, and he wanted his family and friends to benefit from what Peter would teach him. Cornelius invited his friends and family to hear Peter, the preacher.

When was the last time you went out of your way, as Peter did, to share God's kindness with others? Peter's obedience to God resulted in answered prayers for Cornelius and an entire family coming to know Christ. We may never know how God uses our daily obedience to Him, as we share His kindness with the world. As you prepare this week, spend time asking God to prepare you, as He prepared Peter to share His kindness. Ask Him to help you see the people around you as people who need Him. Like Cornelius, do not be afraid to ask God to send people to you who can teach you more about Him as well.

GOD SHOWS KINDNESS, SO I CAN BE KIND.

WELCOME

ACTIVITY 1: REACTION TIME

MATERIALS: Yardstick

DIRECTIONS: Hold the yardstick with the higher numbers on top. Let kids check their response time by dropping the yardstick through their opened thumb and forefinger. The number where the yardstick is caught is the child's reaction number. The lower the number, the faster the reaction.

CAMPFIRE CONNECTION:

- Who had the fastest reaction time?
- How soon do you react when you see someone in need?

Here are some scenarios you can present to your kids to help them determine their kindness-reaction time.

- When you see someone with their hands full coming towards a door, how quick are you to show kindness by opening the door?
- When you see someone sitting by themselves, how quick are you to show kindness by joining them?
- If you know someone who does not know about Jesus, how quick are you to tell them about Jesus?

Our Bible story today is about someone who had a slow reaction time. Peter did not want to tell Cornelius about Jesus at first, because he was different. He was a Roman, and the Jews did not like the Romans at all. Thankfully, Peter soon understood that everyone needs Jesus, and the kindest thing we can do, as Christians, is to tell others about Him.

ACTIVITY 2: MEMORY VERSE MIX UP

MATERIALS: Different colored papers, Markers, Scissors, White butcher paper

DIRECTIONS: As kids enter, have them draw the memory verse on different colored sheets of paper one or two words at a time. For example, "The" could be drawn on red paper, "fruit" on yellow, "of the" on blue, etc.

When kids have finished drawing out the memory verse, have them cut out the words and mix up the pieces. Let them work in groups to put the verse in order several times. When kids have finished playing with their puzzle, have them paste the pieces onto a white sheet of butcher paper to make a huge memory verse poster.

CAMPFIRE CONNECTION:

It took all kinds of colors to make this poster look great. In the same way, it takes a lot of different kinds of people to make up the beautiful world God made. God made each one of us to be different in our own special way. He made you, and loves you, just the way you are. God also made the person next to you and the people all around the world! God shows His kindness to each of us, and He wants us to be kind to everyone we meet.

- How has God shown His kindness to you?

Today's Bible lesson is about Peter and Cornelius. Peter did not want to tell Cornelius about Jesus, because he was a Roman soldier. But God wants us to be kind to everyone. Telling someone about Jesus is the kindest thing you can do for a person.

- Have you ever done something kind for someone who is not like you?
- What are some ways you can show kindness to others?

God never fails to be kind, and neither should we. Everything we do should point straight back to God's unfailing kindness and everlasting love for people.

BIBLE LESSON

GOD SHOWS KINDNESS, SO I CAN BE KIND.

INTRO

In Galatians 5:22-23, Paul talks about some of the ways knowing God shows up in our lives. He calls these ways the fruit of the Spirit. We are learning about the fruit of the Spirit by studying some of the first Christians, the first people to have the Holy Spirit living inside of them. Today we are going to learn about the ways God shows us kindness.

STICKER STOP

Place the Kindness Sticker on your Fruit of the Spirit poster *(See page 5).*

Can anyone remember a time when someone did something kind for you? Maybe your mom or dad helped you clean your room, or a new friend included you in a game on the playground? It feels great when someone goes out of their way to show us kindness.

Remember, the fruit of the Spirit comes from knowing God and allowing His character to "rub off" on us. Let's think of ways God shows His kindness to us. *(He sent Jesus, He listens to us and answers our prayers, He provides for us, He blesses us with even more than we need sometimes, etc.)*

This sticker has a lot of arrows pointing up. The arrows on the kindness sticker remind us that everything we do should point straight to God. The way we speak and act towards others should always be kind. Our kindness can point others to Christ.

In today's Bible story, God showed His kindness to Peter and a Roman soldier named Cornelius. Then, because He knew and listened to God, Peter chose to share God's kindness with Cornelius.

READ THE BIBLE

Before we get started on this story, it is important to remember that Peter was a Jew. Jews did not like the Romans. They especially did not like Roman soldiers. Because Rome had taken over Israel, the law allowed Roman soldiers to stay wherever they wanted, whenever they wanted. Imagine if one day a soldier from another country made you move out of your room for two weeks, cook for him and wait on him hand-and-foot! You would probably be upset, right? In addition, Roman soldiers were allowed to force people to carry their heavy bags for a mile in any direction. If a soldier asked you to carry his bag, it did not matter if you were late to school, sick, or already had your hands full. By law, you had to stop what you were doing and carry his things!

Open your Bibles to Acts 10. Cornelius was a very important Roman soldier. He loved God and treated others well. He did not know much about God, but he prayed and gave money to the Jewish people. In Acts 10, the Lord spoke to Cornelius, telling him to send messengers to Joppa to find Peter. Meanwhile Peter was in Joppa, on the roof of his house praying.

Read Acts 10:10-16.

What in the world? Three times, Peter saw a vision of animals on a sheet. They were animals Jews were not supposed to eat, but God told him to eat them anyway. Peter was confused about the vision. Just then, Cornelius' messengers arrived. The Lord told Peter to go with them to Cornelius' house.

Remember, Cornelius was a Roman soldier. Even though he did not understand, Peter obeyed God and went to Cornelius' house. Before the vision, Peter might not have gone. He thought Jesus had come for the Jews only. Now Peter understood Jesus came for everyone. He understood now that everyone needed to know the Good News about Jesus.

Peter went to Cornelius' house in Joppa. The Bible tells us Cornelius had invited his family and friends to hear about God. He was excited to hear what Peter had to say about God.

PRESENT THE GOSPEL

Even though Peter and Cornelius were very different, Peter showed Cornelius God's kindness. He told the Roman soldier and his whole family that God, in His kindness, did not leave us to pay the punishment for our sins. Instead, God sent His only Son, Jesus, to die on the cross and take the punishment that we deserve for all of the wrong choices we have made and will make in the future. Jesus came back to life three days after He was buried and is alive today.

Because of Jesus' kindness, because of His sacrifice, we can have a relationship with God. Admit that you have sinned. Tell God you are sorry for your wrong thoughts, words, and actions. Ask Him to forgive you. Tell Him you believe that Jesus is the Son of God, who died and rose again. Then, put God in charge of your life. Ask Him to take over and teach you how to live His way.

APPLICATION

Read Acts 10:44-48.

When Cornelius heard this, he and everyone in his house believed. They started a relationship with God, and the Holy Spirit came to live in them. Peter baptized everyone who believed as a picture of the new life they had because of Jesus.

Telling people the Good News about Jesus is the kindest thing we can do, because we are introducing them to a relationship with our loving, joyful, peaceful, patient, and kind God. When was the last time you told someone the Good News about Jesus? Or like Cornelius, when was the last time you invited others to come with you to hear the Good News about Jesus in church? Jesus is the best news the world has ever received. It is our job, as Christians, to tell the world that Jesus, God's Son, came to earth to take our punishment, so we can be friends with God. So don't wait. Tell someone about Him today!

When was the last time you were kind to someone who was not kind to you? Peter was kind to Cornelius even though he was a Roman soldier. The two men were very different and probably disagreed on many things. But Peter obeyed God. Now they both agreed on at least one very important thing: Jesus is Lord! That is amazing! I challenge you this week to pray for the people who are mean to you or different from you. Ask God to show His kindness to them through you and others, too.

PRAY

ACTIVITY 3: ELEVATING KINDNESS

MATERIALS: Balloons

DIRECTIONS: Split your class into four groups and have them spread out in circles. Each group needs to choose one person to "elevate." This person stands in the middle of the circle. Kids in the group must think of kind words or actions they can say or do for the person being "elevated." Kids write these ideas or words on balloons and toss them to the middle of the circle. The "elevated" person hits them to other people in the group while saying other kind things to those in the circle. As time allows, let different kids be "elevated."

CAMPFIRE CONNECTION:

- Was it easy to keep thinking of new things to write on the balloons?
- How do your words and actions lift up others?
- How would you feel if someone came up to you and tried to pop one of your balloons?
- What kind of words or actions could pop someone's balloon (tear them down)?

Kindness comes in many forms. We can choose to be kind with our words and with our actions. However we choose to show kindness, we can be sure it will lift others up. When you are making choices, ask yourself, "Is what I'm about to say or do going to lift that person up or tear them down?"

GOD SHOWS KINDNESS, SO I CAN BE KIND.

ACTIVITY 4: MISSIONARY TAG

MATERIALS: None

DIRECTIONS: Line kids up against one wall in the classroom. Choose one person to be the Missionary. Kids try to get from one wall to the other without being tagged by the Missionary. When tagged by the Missionary, kids also become Missionaries. (The game is played much like sharks and minnows.) Play the game a few times, so everyone gets a chance to be a Missionary.

CAMPFIRE CONNECTION:

The arrows on the kindness sticker remind us that everything we do should point straight to God! The way we speak and act toward others should always be kind. Our kindness can point others to Christ.

- Discuss different ways you can show kindness to your family, friends, or a stranger. (Have kids do this discussion in pairs, so everyone participates.)

ACTIVITY 5: FOLLOW THE LEADER

MATERIALS: None

DIRECTIONS: Choose one person to be the Leader. The Leader can make silly actions or walk around the room, and everyone else must copy them. Play this a few times to make sure everyone gets a chance to be the Leader.

CAMPFIRE CONNECTION:

God wants us to be kind to others, because He is kind to us. We are to follow His example, just like we followed the Leader in our game.

- How does Jesus show kindness?
- How can you copy what Jesus did?
- Why do you think Jesus wants us to be kind to one another?
- How can you lead others to Jesus with kindness?

MEMORY VERSE: GALATIANS 5:22-23

MATERIALS: "Fruit of the Spirit" song (several versions of this song can be found online via YouTube and other streaming services), Music player

DIRECTIONS: Write the memory verse on the board for everyone to see. Read the verse together. Play the song for your class. Teach fun motions to go with each characteristic of the fruit or let your class make up their own fun motions.

CAMPFIRE CONNECTION:

When a tree is healthy, it gives off fruit. Apple trees give apples, pear trees give pears, and pine trees give pine cones. What does a healthy and growing Christian give? *(The fruit of the Spirit of God!)* As we grow in our friendship with God, we begin to become more like Him.

Today, we learned about the ways God's kindness rubs off on us.

- How does God show kindness to us?
- What can we do to share God's kindness with others?
- How did Peter share God's kindness with Cornelius?

"But the fruit of the Spirit is love, joy, peace, patience, kindness, goodness, faithfulness, gentleness, self control; against such things there is no law."

GALATIANS 5:22-23

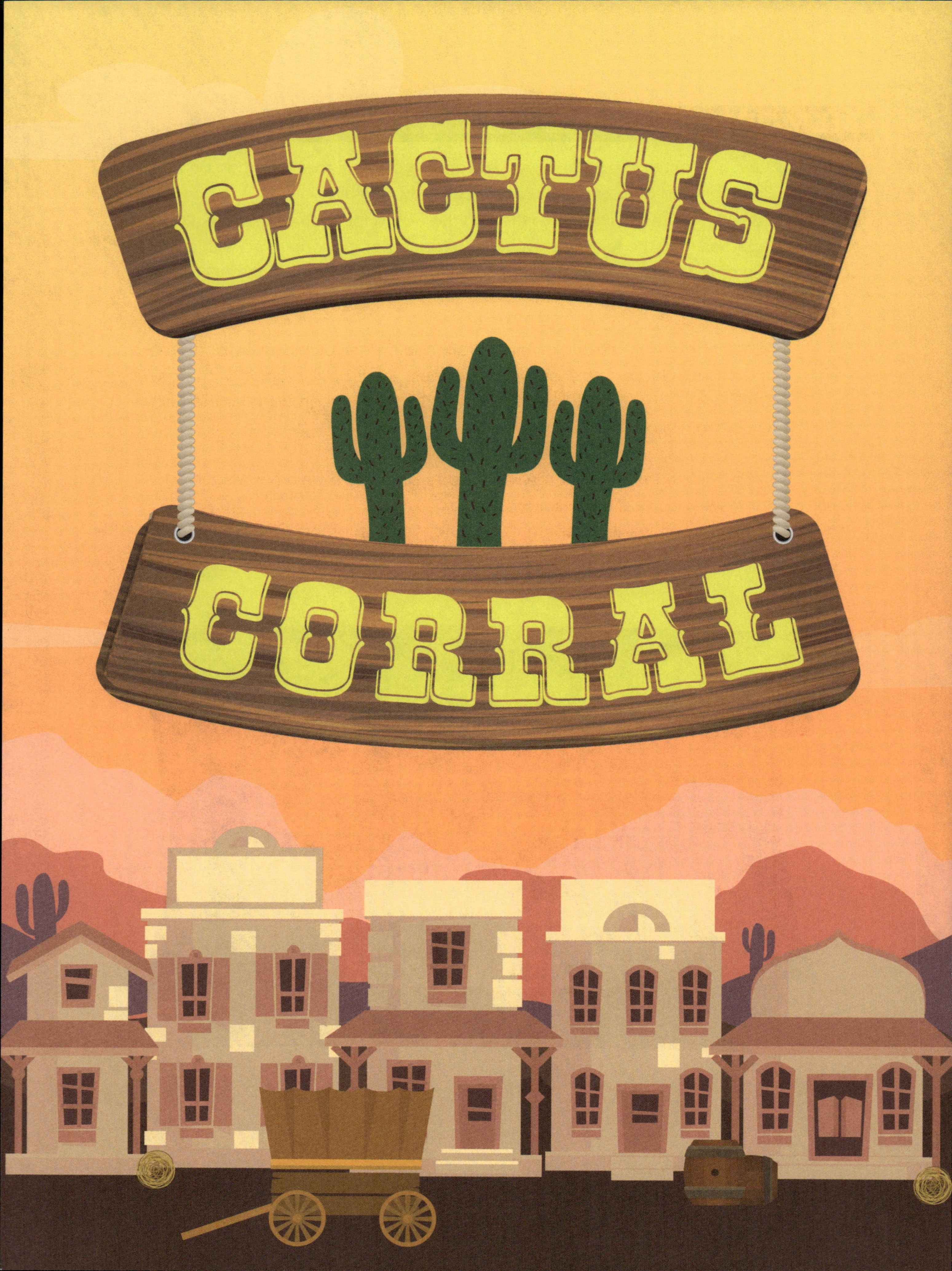
CACTUS
CORRAL

LESSON 6

MAIN POINT

God Shows Goodness,
so I Can Be Good.

BIBLE STORY

Dorcas Is Raised from the Dead.
(Acts 9:32-43)

MEMORY VERSE

"But the fruit of the Spirit is love, joy, peace, patience, kindness, goodness, faithfulness, gentleness, self control; against such things there is no law." Galatians 5:22-23 [NASB]

DON'T BE A PRICKLY PEAR!

SUPPLIES FROM THE GENERAL STORE

Activity 1:
On the Lookout activity sheet

Activity 2:
Paper, Ticky-Tak, Masking or velcro tape

Activity 3:
Origami Goodness Square

Bible Lesson:
Fruit of the Spirit poster (See page 5) and Goodness sticker

Object Lesson 1:
Camera with flash, Flashlight

Object Lesson 2:
Musical instrument

Memory Verse:
"Fruit of the Spirit" song, (several versions of this song can be found online via YouTube and other streaming services) Music player

LEADER DEVOTION

READ

Acts 9:32-43

By the account in Acts 9, Dorcas saw the needs around her and looked for ways to do good. She was known for her good deeds and was greatly missed when she died. Widows brought in clothing and blankets she had made for them, asking nothing in return. Dorcas understood Paul's words in **Galatians 6:9-10, "So let's not get tired of doing what is good. At just the right time we will reap a harvest of blessing if we don't give up. Therefore, whenever we have the opportunity, we should do good to everyone – especially to those in the family of faith."**

As adopted sons and daughters of God, it is important that we remember why we do good. We do good, because we personally know and serve a good God. Our good deeds, our works, come from an overflow of our relationship with the Lord. In no way do our deeds form that relationship. In other words, there is nothing we can do that will make Him love us more, and there is nothing we can do that will make Him love us less. God loves us with the full extent of His love.

Our good deeds do, however, help us communicate His love to a world in need. Between 250 and 270 AD, a plague ravished Rome. Emperor Decius seized the opportunity to blame the Christians. Christians seized the opportunity to do good, to spread the love of Christ. While doctors and officials fled the cities, Christians stayed behind to minister to the sick, often dying alongside their pagan neighbors. When the world saw this, many came to Christ as a direct result of their selflessness.

What would the world be like if we stopped to assess the needs around us and the extent to which we could meet those needs? Take Paul's challenge from Galatians. Do not wait to do good. Do good while you have the opportunity to do so. Then we will "reap" the benefits of living as His hands and feet on this earth, as we share His love with those around us.

WELCOME

ACTIVITY 1: ON THE LOOKOUT ACTIVITY SHEET

MATERIALS: On the Lookout activity sheet (page 105)

DIRECTIONS: Have kids look for each of the listed items on the sheet. The first person to find all of the items wins.

CAMPFIRE CONNECTION:

We see a lot of things every day. Just today you probably saw people in the cars next to you as you rode to church. You saw people walking to church with you this morning. You saw your family. Right now, you see your friends. This afternoon, you might see someone walking on the side of the road. Maybe you will see someone who is homeless. Or maybe when you turn on the TV, you'll see people from different parts of the world who are hurting or in trouble.

The fruit of the Spirit that we will learn about today is GOODNESS. How can we help the people that we see every day? (Ex. Hold the door open, smile, say something nice, etc.) It starts with looking for opportunities around us. Just like you looked very hard for some of the items in the On the Lookout activity sheet, we should also look hard for opportunities to do good to others!

ACTIVITY 2: MEMORY VERSE MIX UP

MATERIALS: Paper, Ticky-Tak, Masking or velcro tape

DIRECTIONS: **Before Class**, make four signs that read Europe / Asia, Africa, North & South America, and Australia. Hang one of these signs in each of the four corners of the room. Tape off boxes around each corner of the room.

During Class, choose one person to be "It". That person stands in the middle of the room. Divide everyone else among the four corners. When you say "Go," everyone must run to a new corner. The person in the middle tries to tag as many people as possible before they reach a new safe zone. Those tagged then join the person in the middle and also try to tag as many people as possible. Play this game a few times, each time allowing someone new to be "It".

CAMPFIRE CONNECTION:

God wants to share His goodness with the world, and He wants to use YOU to do it.

- How was the person in the middle (It) like a missionary?
- How can you share God's goodness with someone in another country?

ACTIVITY 3: ORIGAMI GOODNESS CRAFT

MATERIALS: Origami Goodness Square (page 107)

DIRECTIONS: Have kids color the paper if they want. Kids then cut out the square and fold along the dotted lines to make the origami game.

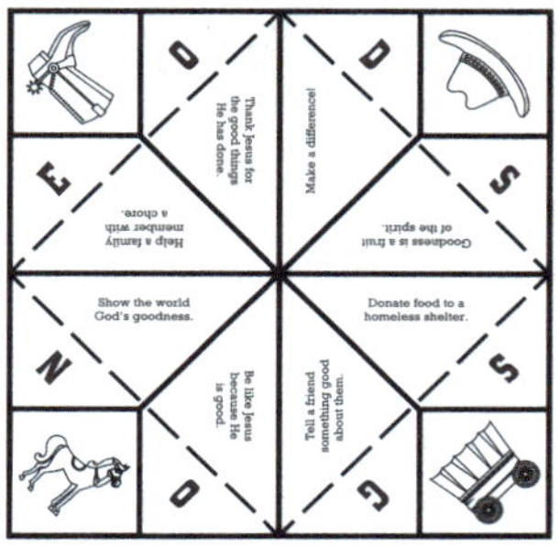

1. Place the square printed side down and fold diagonally into a triangle.
2. Fold diagonally again into a smaller triangle.
3. Unfold all of the folds, and open the square back up, printed side down.
4. Fold one corner into a center point. Do this for all four corners. This will result in a smaller square. Turn it over so the pictures are face down.
5. Fold a corner to the center point. Do this for all the rest of the corners. This will result in a smaller square.
6. With the pictures face down, fold the square in half. Unfold and fold in half the other way to create crease lines.
7. Pick up each of the 4 square flaps and put your fingers inside (The flaps have pictures printed on them.)

CAMPFIRE CONNECTION:

Sharing God's goodness with others can be fun. Let's play the game to help us choose what good thing we can do right now!

BIBLE LESSON

GOD SHOWS GOODNESS, SO I CAN BE GOOD.

INTRO

In Galatians 5:22-23, Paul talks about some of the ways knowing God shows up in our lives. He calls these things the fruit of the Spirit. We are learning about the fruit of the Spirit by studying some of the first Christians, the first people to have the Holy Spirit living inside of them. Today we are going to learn about the ways that God shows us goodness.

STICKER STOP

Place the Goodness Sticker on your Fruit of the Spirit poster *(See page 5).*

Remember, the fruit of the Spirit comes from knowing God and allowing His character to "rub off" on us. Let's think of ways that God shows His goodness to us.

This sticker has a person with binoculars looking out. Today we are learning we should always be on the lookout to do something good. Our Bible story today is about a lady named Dorcas. Can you imagine having that name? Even though she had a really unusual name, the thing that stood out most about Dorcas was the good she did for others.

Have you ever been to a funeral? It's a sad question to start out with, but our lesson today is about a funeral that had a happy ending.

- What happened at the funeral you attended?
- How did people act at the funeral?
- What kind of things did people say about the person who died?

READ THE BIBLE

Read Acts 9:36-37.

People who knew Dorcas were very sad when she died, because Dorcas was a good person. She was always doing something good for other people.

- Do you know someone in your life who is like Dorcas? Who always looks for good things to do for others?

Let's see what happened at the rest of the funeral. **Read Acts 9:38-43.**

- What kind of things did people have to say about Dorcas? (Acts 9:39)

Wow! Dorcas really knew what it meant to show God's goodness. We should share God's goodness with the people around us like Dorcas did. **Be a Dorcas!**

The people who knew Dorcas were really sad when she died. She showed other people the goodness of God through her good deeds for them. When she died, everyone was so sad. They asked Peter to pray and ask God to bring her back to life. God used Peter to raise Dorcas back to life! I bet no one has EVER been to a funeral that ended that way!

- Think about the people you know who do good things for other people. How are these people like Jesus? How does Jesus show us His goodness?

PRESENT THE GOSPEL

Jesus was good to everyone He met. He healed the sick and fed the hungry. Jesus even raised people from the dead! But the most amazing thing that Jesus ever did, He did for you and for me! Jesus never did anything wrong - not even one little thing. Jesus knew all of us have made choices we know are wrong. He knows all of us have sinned. Jesus also knew the punishment for sin is death. Each one of us deserves death because of the wrong things we have done. But Jesus did the BEST, most good thing, that anyone could ever do. He decided to take our punishment for us. Jesus died on a cross so that we could be forgiven for our sins. Then three days later, He came back to life! Now we can ask Jesus to forgive us for our sins and choose to make Him the Boss of our lives.

APPLICATION

Dorcas knew the goodness of Jesus, and she shared it with the world through her good deeds. She did good things for lots of people.

- How can you be a Dorcas? In other words, what are some good things that YOU can do for someone else?
- Start out by thinking of good things you can do for your family. What can you do to serve your family? Your friends?
- How can you help the people in your school? Your city? Your world?

PRAY

BE A DORCAS! ALWAYS BE ON THE LOOKOUT FOR SOMETHING GOOD TO DO!

OBJECT LESSON 1: FLASHLIGHT GOODNESS

MATERIALS: Camera with flash, Flashlight
DIRECTIONS: Get everyone together for a class picture. Be sure to use the flash when you take the picture. Once everyone sits down, turn on a flashlight.

- What's the difference between the light a flashlight gives and the light that comes from a camera flash?

The flash is here and gone in an instant, but the flashlight keeps giving off bright light. God has given us goodness. He doesn't want us to show His goodness just every once in a while. God wants us to live a consistently bright life for Him.

OBJECT LESSON 2: MUSICAL GOODNESS

MATERIALS: Musical instrument
DIRECTIONS: Have someone who does not know how to play the instrument try to play. Then hand it off to someone who can play.

- Why did the second person sound better when they played?

Just holding an instrument doesn't make you a skilled musician. You have to practice. In the same way, God has given each of us His goodness. It may feel awkward at first, when you do good things for others. But don't worry. The more you practice sharing the goodness of Jesus, the easier it will become. We must use God's goodness daily for others to see the beautiful music from God in our lives.

GOD SHOWS GOODNESS, SO I CAN BE GOOD.

MEMORY VERSE: GALATIANS 5:22-23

MATERIALS: "Fruit of the Spirit" song (several versions of this song can be found online via YouTube and other streaming services), Music player

DIRECTIONS: Write the memory verse on the board for everyone to see. Read the verse together. Play the song for your class. Teach fun motions to go with each characteristic of the fruit or let your class make up their own fun motions.

CAMPFIRE CONNECTION:

When a tree is healthy, it gives off fruit. Apple trees give apples, pear trees give pears, and pine trees give pine cones. What does a healthy and growing Christian give? *(The fruit of the Spirit of God!)* As we grow in our friendship with God, we begin to become more like Him.

Today we learned about the ways that God's goodness rubs off on us.

- How does God show goodness to us?
- What can we do to share God's goodness with others?
- Why should we be on the lookout for opportunities to do good to others?

"But the fruit of the Spirit is love, joy, peace, patience, kindness, goodness, faithfulness, gentleness, self control; against such things there is no law."

GALATIANS 5:22-23

LESSON 7

MAIN POINT

God Is Faithful, so I Can
Be Faithful to Him.

BIBLE STORY

The Church at Antioch Are Called
"Christians." (Acts 11:19-26)

MEMORY VERSE

"But the fruit of the Spirit is love, joy, peace, patience, kindness, goodness, faithfulness, gentleness, self control; against such things there is no law." Galatians 5:22-23 [NASB]

DON'T BE A PRICKLY PEAR!

SUPPLIES FROM THE

GENERAL STORE

Activity 1:

Stickers

Activity 2:

None

Bible Lesson:

Fruit of the Spirit poster (See page 5) and Faithfulness sticker

Activity 3:

Scenarios

Memory Verse:

Memory verse printed out on different colored papers,

Scissors, Glue or tape, White paper

LEADER DEVOTION

READ

Acts 11:19-26

Even under great persecution, the church at Antioch thrived. The city of Antioch was home to about two hundred thousand people at this time in history. The third city of Rome, Antioch played a vital role in the growth of the early church. Paul spent about a year in Antioch teaching Greeks about Jesus and raising up disciples. Paul started his missionary journeys from the church in Antioch.

When Barnabas first came from Jerusalem to see what was happening at this church, he immediately noticed the grace of God. The people's relationship with Christ was so noticeable that the pagans in Antioch gave the Christ followers the name "Christian," meaning "little Christ." The church at Antioch was living by the Spirit, and the fruit of the Spirit was noticeable in their lives. Their defining characteristic was their faithfulness to Jesus.

Think through your life. What is your defining characteristic? If an outsider were to give you a name, what would it be? We pray those around us will immediately notice the grace of God and the power of the Spirit living in us.

Now think through all you know of the Father. How has He shown His faithfulness to you personally? To us generally? I challenge you this week to study the times the word "faithful" or "faithfulness" appears in the Bible. His faithfulness to us is overwhelming. As with all the other characteristics of the fruit of the Spirit of God, we cannot out-faithful Him. We cannot out-love Him, have or give more joy, peace, and patience, or show more kindness and goodness than He does. He will always be faithful to His promises and to His children.

As you study this week, pray God will build faithfulness to Him in your life, so your relationship with Him becomes your defining characteristic.

WELCOME

ACTIVITY 1: STICKER TAG

MATERIALS: Stickers

DIRECTIONS: Hand one child a pack of stickers. In this version of tag, "It" tries to put stickers on as many people as possible before time runs out. If "It" places a sticker on you, you cannot remove it until the game is over. After about 30 seconds, call time and have everyone sit down where they are. The person with the least stickers is "It" for the next round.

CAMPFIRE CONNECTION:

- Did the stickers always stick to your clothes?
- "It," how did you feel when you stuck a note to someone that fell off later?
- What does it mean to stick to Jesus? Can you give a real life example?
- Is it always easy to stick to Jesus? Why/why not?

God is faithful to us. No matter what, God still chooses to love us. He makes the sun rise each morning and set each night. He makes rain fall from the sky to water the plants. He chooses to love us and take care of us even when we choose to sin (Romans 5:8). Today we will learn that we can be faithful to God, because He is faithful to us.

GOD IS FAITHFUL, SO I CAN BE FAITHFUL TO HIM.

ACTIVITY 2: THE NAME GAME

MATERIALS: None

DIRECTIONS: Have kids sit in a circle. Take turns playing the Name Game with each other's name. Here's an example using the name Katie.

"Katie, Katie, bo-batie
Banana-fana fo-fatie
Fee-fi-mo-matie
Katie!"

CAMPFIRE CONNECTION:

Lots of parents name their children after something or someone. For instance, you might be named after a favorite grandmother or television character. Other parents pick a name for their children based on what the name means.

- Do you know what your name means? Are you named after someone?

Back in Bible times, parents waited to name their children until they knew a little about their personality. For example, Barnabas' name means "encourager." He was always encouraging others. In fact, Barnabas was encouraging the people in Antioch in our story today!

- Have you ever wondered where followers of Jesus got the name "Christians?"

Our lesson today is all about how people who believe in Jesus came to be named "Christians."

BIBLE LESSON

GOD IS FAITHFUL, SO I CAN BE FAITHFUL TO HIM.

INTRO

In Galatians 5:22-23, Paul talks about some of the ways knowing God shows up in our lives. He calls these things the fruit of the Spirit. We are learning about the fruit of the Spirit by studying some of the first Christians, the first people to have the Holy Spirit living inside of them. Today, we are going to learn about the ways that God shows us faithfulness.

STICKER STOP

Place the Faithfulness Sticker on your Fruit of the Spirit poster *(See page 5)**.*

Remember, the fruit of the Spirit comes from knowing God and allowing His character to "rub off" on us. Let's think of ways God shows His faithfulness to us.

This sticker looks very gooey and sticky. God is faithful to us. He sticks to His promises no matter what. As Christians, we should "stick to" Jesus!

READ THE BIBLE

Read Acts 11:19-21.

- Do you know what the word "persecution" means? *[Persecution – "subjected to hostility or ill treatment , esp. because of their...religious beliefs" (www.dictionary.com)]*

People who chose to believe in Jesus were being persecuted. Some were beaten. Others were killed – all because they chose to follow Jesus with their lives. But even with all of this, the believers continued to stick by Jesus. They were FAITHFUL to Jesus. The believers were traveling all around, trying to tell as many people as possible the truth about Jesus.

PRESENT THE GOSPEL

Do you know the Good News about Jesus? The truth is every one of us, myself included, have sinned. In other words, we have all chosen to do something we know is wrong. Every time we sin, it separates us from God. That's bad news. But here's the Good News: Jesus, God's Son, came to earth from Heaven to save us. Jesus loved us SO much He came, lived a perfect life, then took our punishment by dying on the cross, even though He had never done anything wrong. Three days later, Jesus came back to life! He is in Heaven now, and He wants to have a relationship with us forever. To have this relationship, we need to first admit we have sinned. Second, we need to believe that Jesus is God's Son, and that He paid the price for our sins. Next, we must choose to follow Him and invite him to be the Boss of our lives. Then, Jesus promises to come into our lives and forgive us for the wrong things we have done! We can have a relationship with Him! Jesus will never leave us! He will be faithful to us for forever! Now that's GOOD NEWS!

READ THE BIBLE

The people living in Antioch knew the Good News about Jesus, and they were SO excited that they wanted to tell EVERYONE about Him no matter what.

Read Acts 11:22-24.

- What did Barnabas notice about the believers living in Antioch? *(The grace of God)*
- What did Barnabas encourage them to do? *("remain true to the Lord with all their hearts")*

Barnabas saw that the believers in Antioch were living for Jesus no matter what. He was excited to see that and encouraged them to stick with Jesus. He encouraged them to stay FAITHFUL to Jesus.

Read Acts 11:25-26.

The word "Christian" literally means "little Christ." The believers at the church of Antioch were acting so much like Jesus that other people started to call them "little Christs!" The non-believers meant it as an insult to the Christians, but as followers of Jesus they took the name as a compliment. The church at Antioch's FAITHFULNESS to Jesus was something that everyone noticed!

Read Acts 1:27-30.

Even when the people around the believers were making fun of them and their beliefs, the Christians still chose to help. God told one of them a famine was coming, so the Christians chose to save their food to help feed the people around them (who were making fun of them). No matter what, they chose to be FAITHFUL to Jesus. They chose to STICK TO Jesus through their actions and words.

APPLICATION

We can be faithful to God, too. Everyone will face a time in life when it would be easier to do what everyone else is doing instead of sticking to Jesus. When that time comes, I challenge you to remember that God is always faithful to His promises. He will be with you. He will give you the strength and the bravery you need to stand up for what you believe.

PRAY

Let's pray together. Let's thank God for keeping all of His promises. Then, let's ask God to help us always be faithful to Him in our thoughts, words, and actions.

GOD IS FAITHFUL, SO I CAN BE FAITHFUL TO HIM.

ACTIVITY 3: STICKY SCENARIOS

MATERIALS: Scenarios

DIRECTIONS: Split your class into four groups. Hand one of the scenarios below to each of the groups. As groups read through the scenarios, encourage everyone to brainstorm ways they can react to the scenario by being faithful to God. To help groups stay focused, have a leader monitor each group. For added fun, have groups act out the various ways they could respond to the scenario.

SCENARIO 1

Your BEST friend invites you to a slumber party for their birthday. You are SO excited! You can't wait to hang out at their house, play fun games, and celebrate your best friend. The day of the party finally comes, and you are having so much fun. When it's time to go to bed, your friend suggests that you watch a movie as you go to sleep. That sounds like fun until you see the movie they want to watch ... Your parents didn't exactly say not to watch it, but you know that it's not a good movie. It's your best friend's BIRTHDAY, and you don't want to make everyone mad. What do you do?

SCENARIO 2

You are convinced that your teacher doesn't like you. Every time someone talks, she blames you, and it seems like she only calls on you when you don't know the answer. After school, you overhear a group of kids in your class making fun of your teacher. After all, she deserves it! It's not like she has been overly nice to you. What do you do?

SCENARIO 3

Your sports team is REALLY good this year. You LOVE playing with your teammates and are getting really excited about the championship game that's coming up. In practice, your coach announces that the championship game will be held in another city on Sunday. Your team will travel there on Saturday afternoon to practice, then play the game on Sunday afternoon. Your coach says if you don't go to practice, you can't play in the game. There's just one problem ... you normally go to church on Sunday. If you go to the game, you'll be missing church. If you go to church, you'll miss the championship game. Your team might lose if you're not there. What do you do?

SCENARIO 4

It has been a really long day, and you are SUPER tired. You normally read your Bible and pray a little before going to bed, but tonight you just feel like going to sleep ... or maybe playing a few short video games before bed. The bottom line is you just don't feel like having your quiet time tonight. What do you do?

CAMPFIRE CONNECTION:

Give kids a little time to complete the assignment, then ask one volunteer from each group to share their scenario and ideas.

- How does the way you chose to react show faithfulness to God?
- Would it be easy to make that choice in real life? Why / why not?
- What could make that choice easier?

If you ever find yourself in a "sticky" scenario, remind yourself that Jesus never leaves you. He will never stop loving you. Jesus sticks with you no matter what! Remembering God's faithfulness to you should make it easier to be faithful to Him in your words and actions.

MEMORY VERSE: GALATIANS 5:22-23

MATERIALS: Memory verse printed out on different colored papers, Scissors, Glue or tape, White paper

DIRECTIONS: Write the memory verse on the board for everyone to see. Read the verse together. Hand out different colored pages with the verse printed on it. Kids cut out each word from the memory verse on the colored paper, then trade with others to make a colorful collage of the memory verse. Let kids paste the individual cut outs onto a sheet of white paper to make a colorful version of the memory verse to take home.

CAMPFIRE CONNECTION:

When a tree is healthy, it gives off fruit. Apple trees give apples, pear trees give pears, and pine trees give pine cones. What does a healthy and growing Christian give? *(The fruit of the Spirit of God!)* As we grow in our friendship with God, we begin to become more like Him.

Today we learned about God's faithfulness.

- How does God show His faithfulness to us?
- What does it mean to be faithful to God?
- How can we be faithful to God in our everyday lives?

"But the fruit of the Spirit is love, joy, peace, patience, kindness, goodness, faithfulness, gentleness, self control; against such things there is no law."

GALATIANS 5:22-23

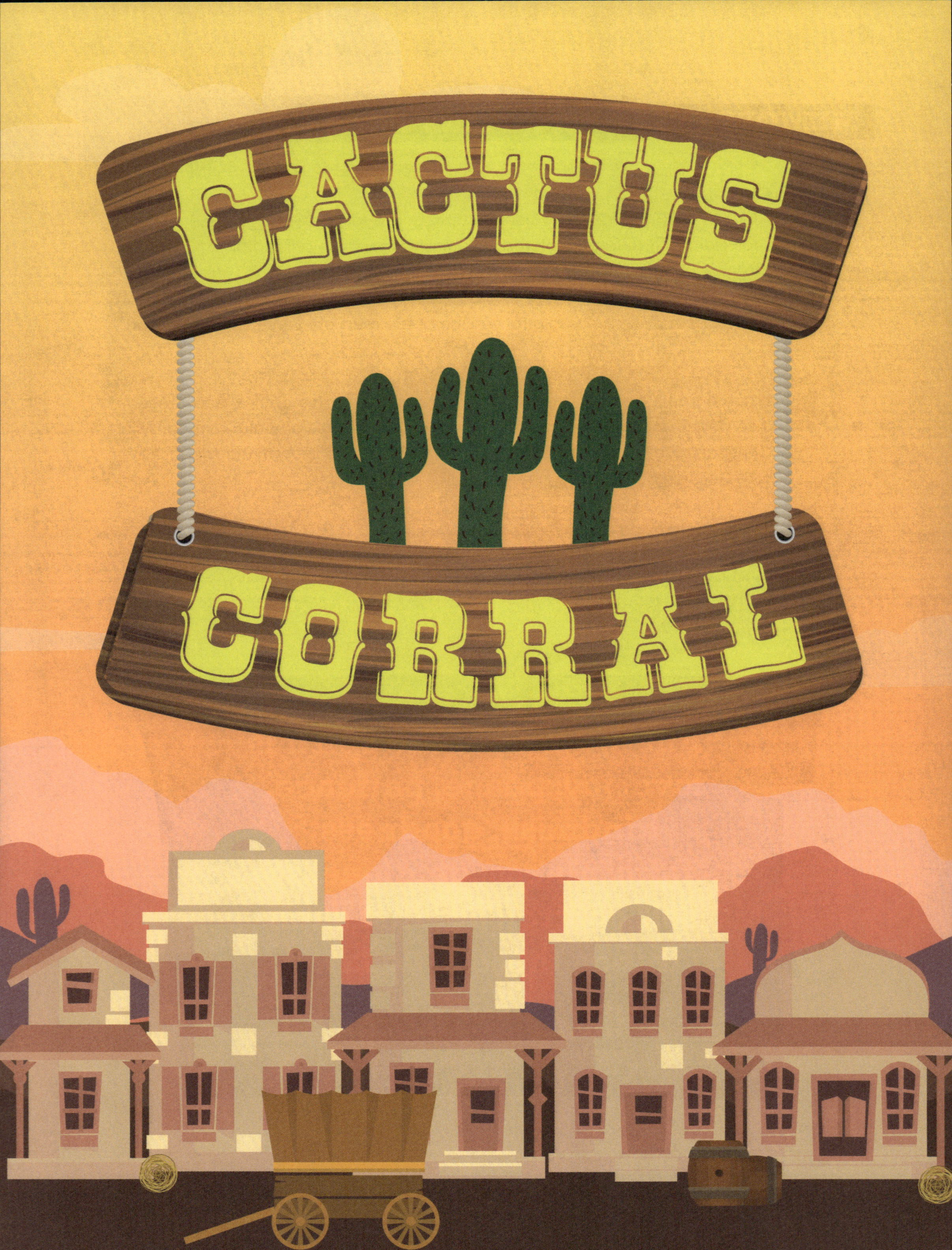
CACTUS
CORRAL

LESSON 8

MAIN POINT

God Shows Gentleness and Self-Control, so I Can Be Gentle and Self-Controlled.

BIBLE STORY

Priscilla and Aquilla Are Gentle with Apollos. (Acts 18:24-28)

MEMORY VERSE

"But the fruit of the Spirit is love, joy, peace, patience, kindness, goodness, faithfulness, gentleness, self control; against such things there is no law." Galatians 5:22-23 [NASB]

DON'T BE A PRICKLY PEAR!

SUPPLIES FROM THE GENERAL STORE

Activity 1:

Bubbles, Toilet paper

Activity 2:

None

Bible Lesson:

Fruit of the Spirit poster (See page 5),

Gentleness and Self-Control stickers

Activity 3:

Scenarios

Memory Verse:

Note cards, Marker, Chairs

LEADER DEVOTION

READ

Acts 18:1-4, 23-28

Priscilla and Aquilla had just enjoyed a year and a half with Paul. They learned about Jesus and were actively telling others about Him, as they lived out a Spirit-led life. When Apollos came, eloquently speaking on only half of the story, Priscilla and Aquilla could have publicly challenged him. They could have chosen to discredit him behind his back, dividing and confusing those who were following Christ. Apollos was wrong, but Priscilla and Aquilla chose to correct him gently by taking him aside to explain the full truth of Christ. Then, they supported him in his ministry. Because of this, Apollos went on to tell many about the Good News of Jesus.

Gentleness is often misunderstood as weakness, when nothing could be further from the truth. Gentleness is strength under control and can only be employed when self-control is at work in our lives. **Proverbs 15:1 says, "A gentle answer deflects anger, but harsh words make tempers flare."** Often we have the power of "right" on our side, but address issues in a way that only stirs up anger and strife. Instead, as **Philippians 4:5 says, "Let everyone see that you are considerate in all you do. Remember, the Lord is coming soon."**

There is great power in our words and actions. With them, we have the power to build up or to destroy (Ephesians 4:29). **2 Timothy 1:7 says, "For God has not given us a spirit of fear and timidity, but of power, love, and self-discipline."** Resolve to bring the conflicts in your life before the Lord first, asking for His wisdom in each case. Ask Him to give you the ability to show a gentle spirit to everyone. Ask Him to grant you self-control as you deal with difficult situations, so He will be glorified in the midst of conflict and in the outcome.

WELCOME

ACTIVITY 1: GENTLENESS STATIONS

MATERIALS: Bubbles, Toilet paper

DIRECTIONS: Set up at least two stations of the bubbles challenge and two stations of the toilet paper challenge. As kids come into class, direct them to one of the stations. After a few minutes, have everyone switch to a new game in the room.

Bubbles Challenge: Let kids take turns seeing how long they can keep a bubble airborne before it pops. The person who keeps the bubble in the air the longest wins.

Toilet Paper Challenge: Choose one person at each station to be wrapped in toilet paper. When you say "go," each group works together to wrap the person in toilet paper. Here's the catch: if the toilet paper breaks, the group has to stop wrapping and sit down. The group that wraps their person with the most toilet paper without breaking any paper wins!

CAMPFIRE CONNECTION:

- What was the best strategy for keeping the bubbles in the air?

You have a lot of power in your breath. If you blow a bubble too hard, it will pop. You had to control your strength in order to win. In the same way, your words hold a lot of power. You have the power to make someone's day or hurt their heart in the words you speak.

- What was the best strategy for keeping the toilet paper in one piece?

Your arms have much more strength than the toilet paper can handle. You could easily rip the toilet paper into several little pieces. In the same way, your actions hold a lot of power. Your actions have the power to make someone's day or hurt someone. Our lesson today is about GENTLENESS. **Gentleness is strength under control.** Control the power of your words and actions by asking God to give you a gentle spirit.

ACTIVITY 2: MEMORY VERSE MIX UP

MATERIALS: None

DIRECTIONS: Choose one child to be the stoplight. Have the rest of your class line up against a wall. The stoplight stands against the opposite wall with their back to the rest of the class.

The stoplight calls out green light, yellow light, or red light. When kids hear "green light", they are allowed to move toward the stoplight. "Yellow light" means move in slow motion, and "red light" means STOP! Anyone who does not follow the instructions right away is sent back to the wall to start over. The first person to reach the stoplight wins and becomes the stoplight for the next round.

CAMPFIRE CONNECTION:

- What happened when you didn't stop right away after hearing red light?
- Whose fault was it, if you didn't follow the instructions right away and were sent back to the wall?

The choices we make have consequences. In other words, our choices have a cost, or penalty. Good choices have good outcomes, but bad choices can really hurt you and others. No one can make your choices but you. Sometimes it's easy to blame other people for the mistakes we make. SELF-CONTROL is realizing YOU are in control of YOU.

So when you are faced with a choice of any kind, think of a stoplight:

RED: Stop. Pause for a short second to make sure you are making a good choice.
YELLOW: Pray. Ask God if you are unsure what you should do.
GREEN: Proceed with caution. Make the choice. But always be mindful of others in each situation. Be gentle.

BIBLE LESSON

GOD SHOWS GENTLENESS AND SELF-CONTROL, SO I CAN BE GENTLE AND SELF-CONTROLLED.

INTRO

In Galatians 5:22-23, Paul talks about some of the ways knowing God shows up in our lives. He calls these things the fruit of the Spirit. We are learning about the fruit of the Spirit by studying some of the first Christians, the first people to have the Holy Spirit living inside of them. Today we are going to learn about the ways that God shows us gentleness and self-control.

STICKER STOP

Place the Gentleness Sticker on your Fruit of the Spirit poster (See page 5).

Remember, the fruit of the Spirit comes from knowing God and allowing His character to "rub off" on us. Let's think of ways that God shows His gentleness to us.

This sticker looks like a sheep. The Bible often compares us to sheep, with Jesus as the Shepherd (John 10). Jesus takes care of us. He cares about us, and always disciplines with love. Just like a shepherd treats his sheep with gentleness, we should be careful when dealing with the people around us. Think about it: you would never pet a sheep with all the strength you have, because you would hurt the sheep. Instead, you would control your strength, because you care about the sheep. Gentleness is strength under control.

Speaking of control, the last fruit of the Spirit is self-control. *Place the Self-Control Sticker on your Fruit of the Spirit poster* (See page 5).

This sticker has a bunch of different controls on it. It would be great if someone else could control us and make sure we were always making good choices. But only YOU are in control of YOU and the choices you make.

In today's Bible story, Priscilla and Aquilla had a choice to make, when they heard someone teaching who did not know the whole truth about Jesus. Listen closely to this true story in the Bible. Priscilla and Aquilla chose to speak and act with gentleness and self-control.

READ THE BIBLE

Read Acts 18:1-4.

Priscilla and Aquilla were friends with Paul. Paul had taught them all about Jesus.

PRESENT THE GOSPEL

He taught them all people are sinners and the punishment for sin is death and separation from God (Romans 6:23). Paul told them Jesus came to earth to take the punishment for our sins, when He died on the cross. Then He defeated death once and for all, when He rose from the dead three days later. Priscilla and Aquilla asked Jesus to forgive them. They believed Jesus was the Son of God and chose to give their whole lives to Him. Because of what Jesus did, you and I can choose to follow Him, too. If you have never asked Jesus to be the Boss of your life, don't put it off!

READ THE BIBLE

Read Acts 18:24-25.

Apollos did not know the whole truth about Jesus. He believed in God, but He didn't know Jesus had paid the price for our sins and was alive again. When Apollos was teaching in the synagogues, he was only telling half of the story. Pricilla and Aquilla knew this when they heard him.

- What are some different ways they could have told him he was wrong?
- What would have been the easiest way?

Read Acts 18:26.

Priscilla and Aquilla could easily have told him he was wrong in front of everyone he was teaching. They could have embarrassed him, but they chose to be GENTLE by inviting him to their house to talk to him in private.

- Have you ever been called out for something in front of others?
- How did that make you feel?

Priscilla and Aquilla understood people's hearts are fragile – they are easily broken. They were very careful when dealing with Apollos' heart.

Read Acts 8:27-28.

Because Priscilla and Aquilla used SELF-CONTROL, and took the time to speak to Apollos in a GENTLE way, Apollos came to understand the truth about Jesus. He started to preach to others the whole truth about Jesus. Apollos even went on mission trips around the world to tell others about the great things Jesus did!

- Do you think Apollos would have believed in Jesus if Priscilla and Aquilla had treated him differently? Why or why not?

Priscilla & Aquilla's gentleness made a powerful impact on Apollos. Apollos then made a powerful impact for God in the world. There is great power in a gentle spirit.

APPLICATION & OBJECT LESSON

Self-control and gentleness are very important. Like Priscilla and Aquilla, we must always remember that people's hearts are fragile.

Draw a large heart on a piece of paper. Hold it up for everyone to see.

Let's say this heart belongs to someone who is making you angry or annoyed. Many times, when someone is annoying us, we want to say something mean in anger. We want to do something annoying or mean back.

Wrinkle the piece of paper with every example you give.

When we do this, it hurts that person's heart. No matter what someone has done to us, we should not purposefully try to hurt others' hearts by our words or actions. Now look at this heart. It is all crumpled up. What will happen when I try to fix it, to straighten the heart back out?

Try to remove the wrinkles in the paper. Show everyone that it cannot be done, then put the paper away.

This is why self-control and gentleness are so important. Our words and actions have consequences for ourselves and others. It is not always easy to use self-control, especially when we know that the other person is wrong. It is especially not easy to show self-control and gentleness when people are making you angry. But like all of the other characteristics of the fruit of the Spirit we have learned, these characteristics come from knowing God and allowing Him to "rub off" on us.

PRAY

Let's pray together. Let's thank God for being gentle and self-controlled with us. Then, let's ask God to help us learn to be gentle with others. Let's ask Him to help us be self-controlled in our thoughts, words, and actions.

GOD SHOWS GENTLENESS AND SELF-CONTROL, SO I CAN BE GENTLE AND SELF-CONTROLLED.

ACTIVITY 3: STICKY SCENARIOS

MATERIALS: Scenarios

DIRECTIONS: Split your class into four groups. Hand one of the scenarios below to each of the groups. As groups read through scenarios, encourage everyone to brainstorm ways they can react to the scenario by being faithful to God. To help groups stay focused, have a leader monitor each group. For added fun, have groups act out the various ways they could respond to the scenario.

SCENARIO 1

Lunch has got to be the BEST part of the day when you are at school! Well, maybe recess is pretty fun, too … But lunch time is really fun, because you get to talk and joke with your friends. One day at lunch, your table starts to play truth or dare. When it's your turn, you choose "dare." So far, the dares have been funny things like "mix your French fries with orange juice and eat it." But when you choose dare, your table dares you to stand on the table and squawk like a chicken. You know it's against the rules to get out of your seat, much less stand on the table … When you pause for a second, your table starts to make fun of you, calling you a real chicken. Then, one of your friends DOUBLE-DOG Dares you to do it. Everyone knows you HAVE to do a DOUBLE-DOG Dare … or do you? What do you do?

SCENARIO 2

You plan a slumber party at your house for some of your friends. You are so excited, because you get to stay up late and have a lot of fun with your friends. When the slumber party comes, everybody decides to play sardines (a backwards version of hide and seek where only one person hides at first). Everybody plays a few times and has a lot of fun, but when it's your turn to hide, your friends decide they don't want to play anymore. They decide not to look for you and instead hang out and talk in your room without you. After a while, you figure it out and come out of hiding. What do you do when you see your friends?

SCENARIO 3

You studied really hard for the English test last Tuesday, and you feel like you probably got a good grade on it. When your teacher passes out the tests, you see that you were right! You got an A+! You are SO excited! When you look around, though, you notice that most everyone else did not do as well as you. The highest grade you can see is a C+. Ouch! Your teacher spends the whole class time lecturing everyone about how important it is to study. Then she lets everyone know that you were the only one to get a good grade. After class, your friends are upset with you for doing well and making them look bad. Some of them start to make fun of you. One guy doesn't say anything – he just waits till the teachers aren't looking and trips you in the hallway. Then in P.E. he "accidentally" kicks you in the back when you are sitting in the bleachers. What do you do?

SCENARIO 4

You have been best friends with Susie since Kindergarten. She is so fun to hang out with and play with! The new girl on your block, Marcie, seems to really like hanging out with her, too. At first, you are excited to have a new friend. But one day when you call Susie to see if she can come over and play, she says she doesn't really want to be your friend anymore. Marcie told her the truth about you, and now she would rather hang out with Marcie. Of course, you have no idea what she is talking about because you don't really know Marcie that well. You realize that Marcie made up a lot of horrible things about you and told all of those lies to your friend, Susie. The next day you see Marcie and Susie hanging out and having fun without you. They see you, whisper to each other, then act like they didn't know you were there. What do you do?

CAMPFIRE CONNECTION:

If you ever find yourself in a tough scenario like these, remind yourself, Jesus never leaves you. He will never stop loving you. Even when we were still sinning, Jesus took our punishment for us by dying on the cross. He didn't have to do that, but He acted out of love for you and for me. If you find yourself in a hard situation, ask Jesus to help you calm down and make the choice that would honor Him.

MEMORY VERSE: FRUIT BASKET TURNOVER

MATERIALS: Fruit of the Spirit cards (pages 109, 111), Chairs

DIRECTIONS: Cut out multiple copies of the Fruit of the Spirit cards and try to evenly distribute them. (For example, you might have five "love" cards and "joy" on another five, etc.) Have kids set up their chairs in a circle facing in. You should have one less chair than players. Hand out one card to each child in your class. The person without a chair stands in the middle and calls out a fruit of the Spirit. Everyone holding a card with that characteristic written on it must switch chairs. The goal is not to get stuck in the middle. The person in the middle can also call out "Fruit Basket Turnover!" to make EVERYONE switch chairs, regardless of what their card says. If you have a small class, give everyone two or three different cards to make the game more fun.

CAMPFIRE CONNECTION:

We have had a lot of fun the past few weeks learning about the fruit of the Spirit. Have everyone say Galatians 5:22-23 with you to review all of the characteristics of the fruit of the Spirit.

Our lesson today is about Gentleness and Self-Control. Gentleness is strength under control, and Self-Control is being in control of yourself – it's just like it sounds.

- How does God show gentleness and self-control?
- Why are gentleness and self-control important?
- How can we learn to be more gentle and self-controlled?

"But the fruit of the Spirit is love, joy, peace, patience, kindness, goodness, faithfulness, gentleness, self control; against such things there is no law."

GALATIANS 5:22-23

GOD SHOWS GENTLENESS AND SELF-CONTROL, SO I CAN BE GENTLE AND SELF-CONTROLLED.

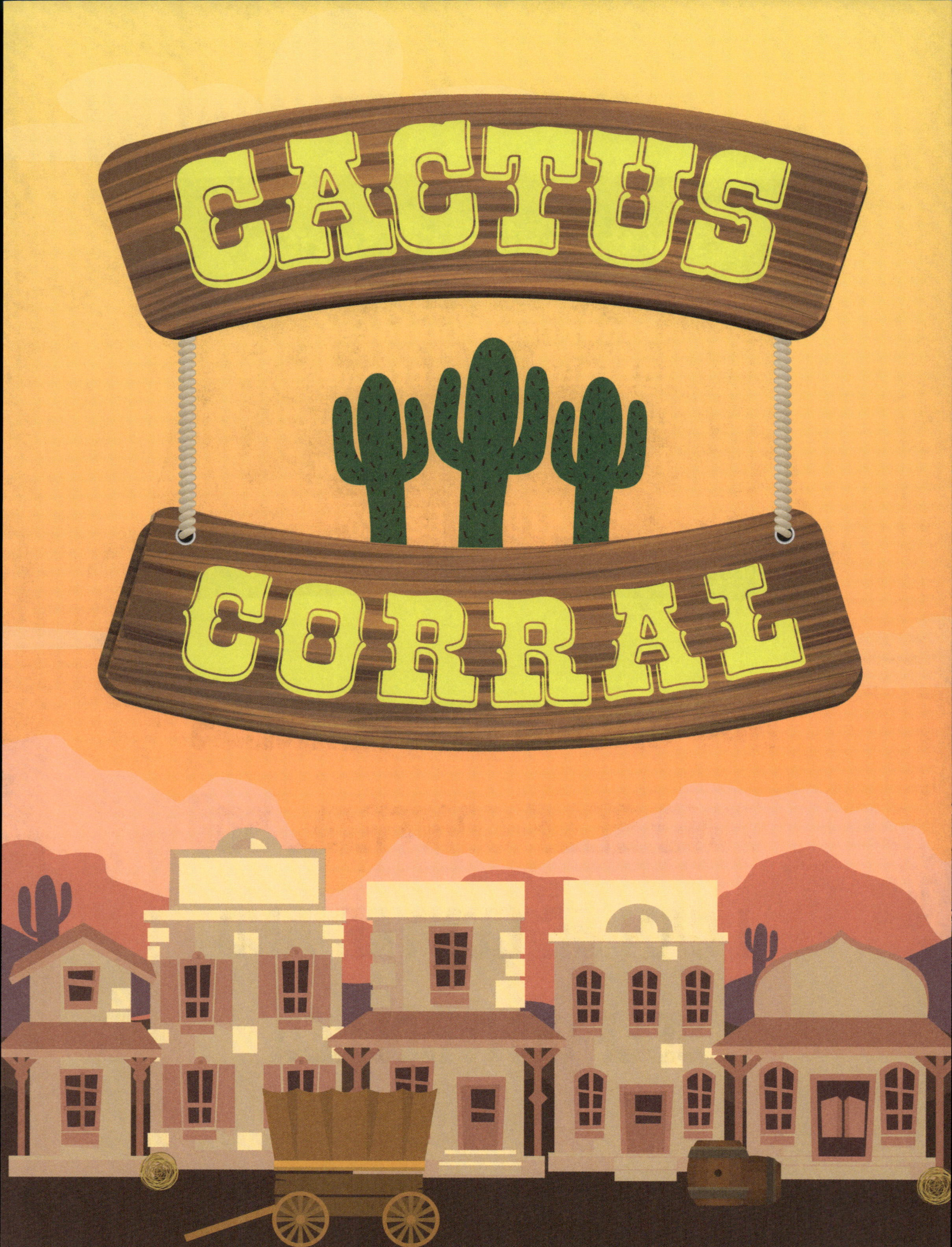
CACTUS
CORRAL

APPENDIX

REPRODUCIBLE PAGES

DON'T BE A PRICKLY PEAR!

ON THE LOOKOUT

From the list below, find each of the items in the picture and fill in the blanks with how many of each you find.

____ Wagon

____ Horse

____ People

____ Helicopter

____ Car

____ Bicycle

____ Motorcycle

____ Airplane

____ Cooking pot

ORIGAMI GOODNESS SQUARE

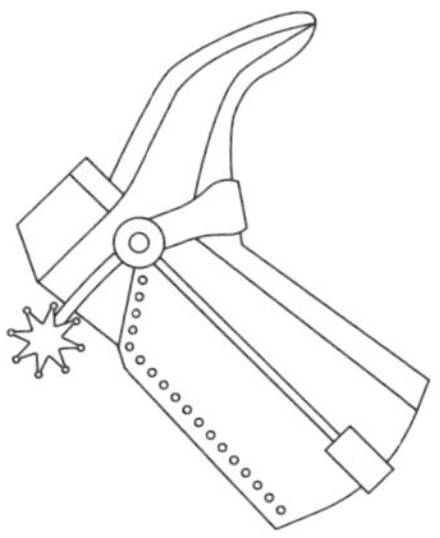

O

D

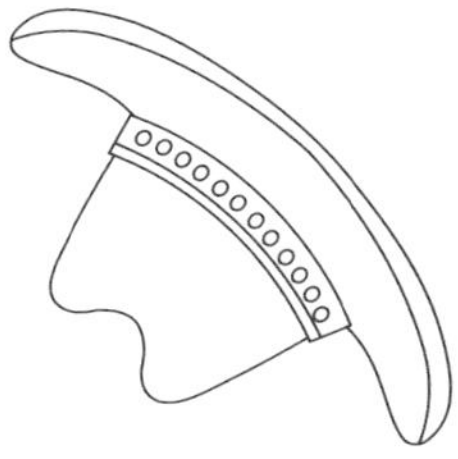

Thank Jesus for the good things He has done.

Make a difference!

E

S

Help a family member with a chore.

Goodness is a fruit of the spirit.

Show the world God's goodness.

Donate food to a homeless shelter.

N

S

Be like Jesus because He is good.

Tell a friend something good about them.

O

G

FRUIT OF THE SPIRIT

LOVE

JOY

PEACE

PATIENCE

KINDNESS

FRUIT OF THE SPIRIT

CACTUS CORRAL

THE FRUIT OF THE SPIRIT COMES FROM KNOWING GOD PERSONALLY AND LEARNING TO LIVE HIS WAY.

Cactus Corral is an eight week study on the fruit of the Spirit as seen in the lives of some of the first Christians in Acts. This series includes leader devotions to help you prepare, western themed games, and engaging Bible lessons that help kids connect to the Bible in a fun and memorable way. In addition, *Cactus Corral* uses interactive visual aids to help kids understand the abstract concept of the fruit of the Spirit.

Lower Elementary Leader Guide
ISBN 9781628629545

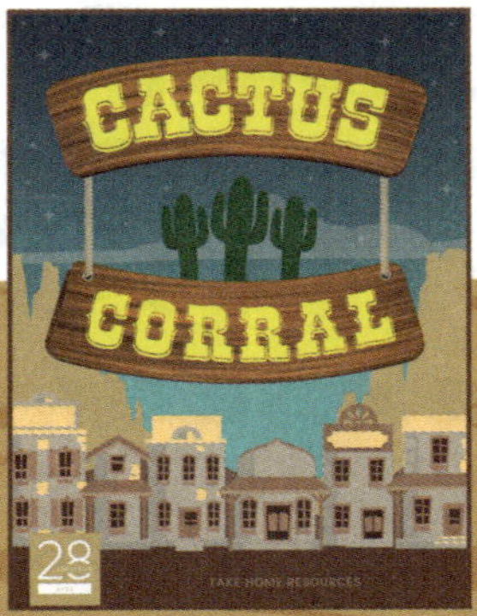

Take Home Resources
ISBN 9781628629569

Upper Elementary Leader Guide
ISBN 9781628629552

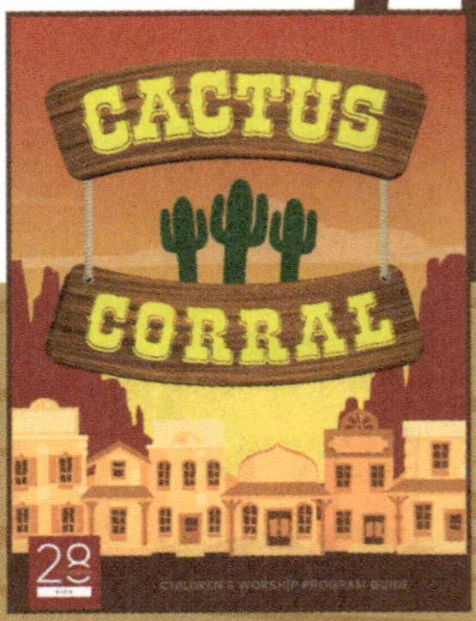

Children's Worship Program Guide
ISBN 9781628629583